GREAT SCOTT!

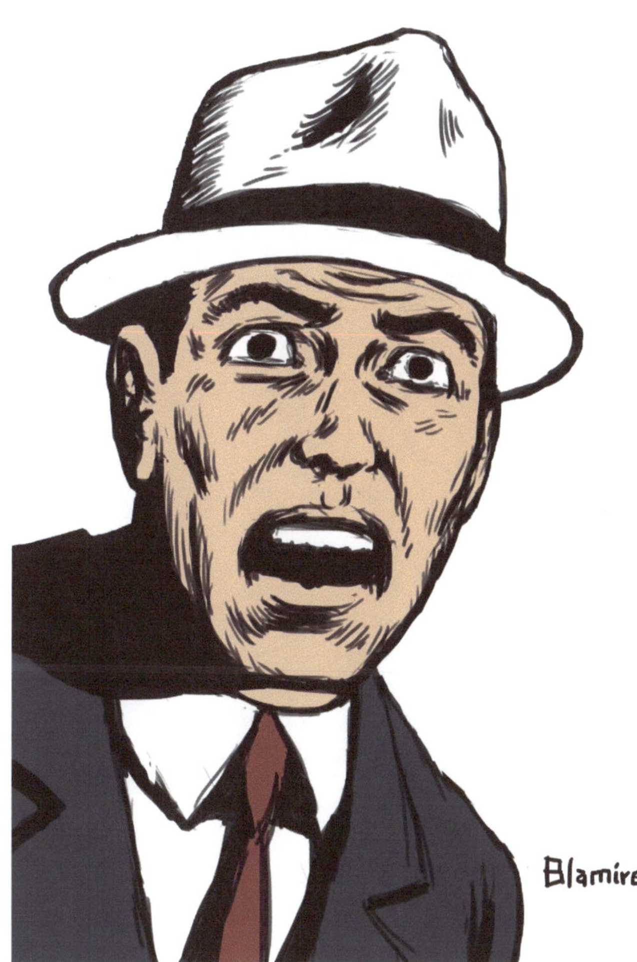

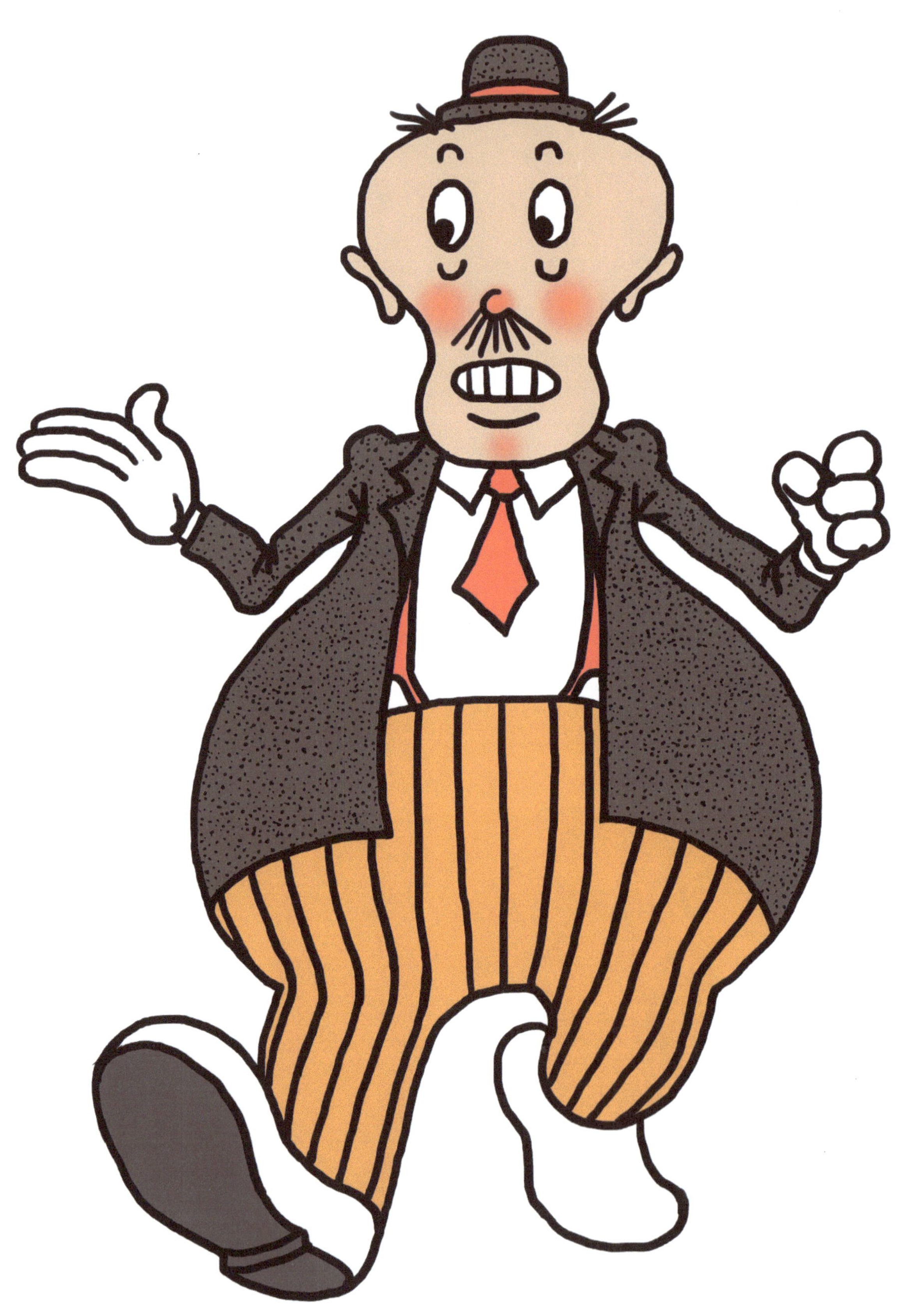

GREAT SCOTT!

the RARE IMAGINARY COMIC BOOK COVERS of Larry Blamire

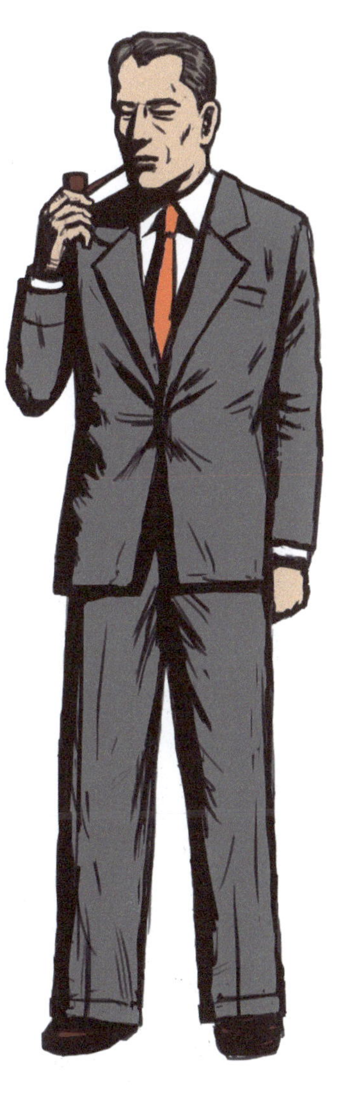

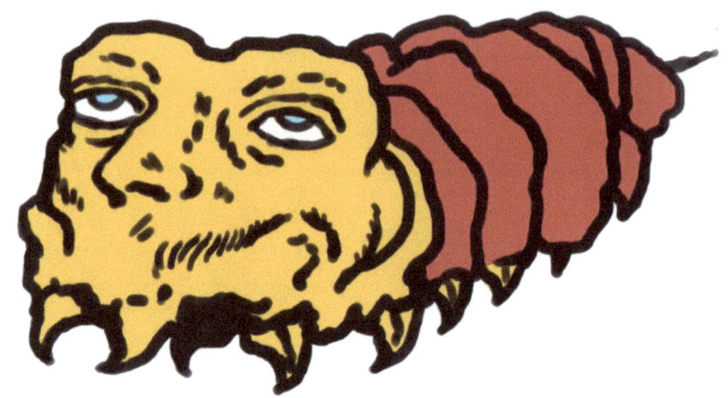

First printing: 2018

ISBN: 978-0-692-18918-4

Bookaroonie Press
bookaroonie@gmail.com

http://www.facebook.com/pages/Larry-Blamire/104521889584067
http://twitter.com/larryblamire/

Cover design by Larry Blamire

All interior art by Larry Blamire

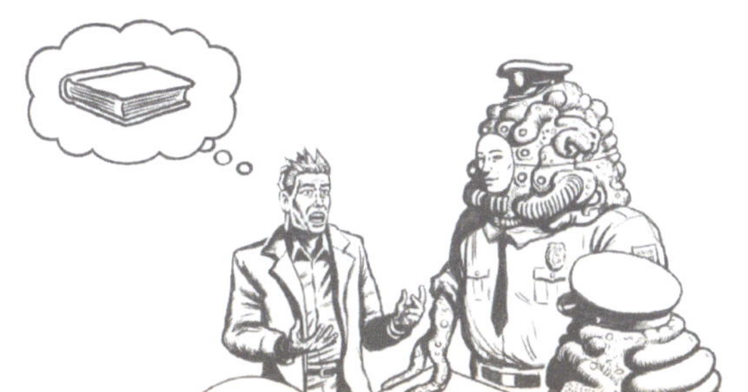

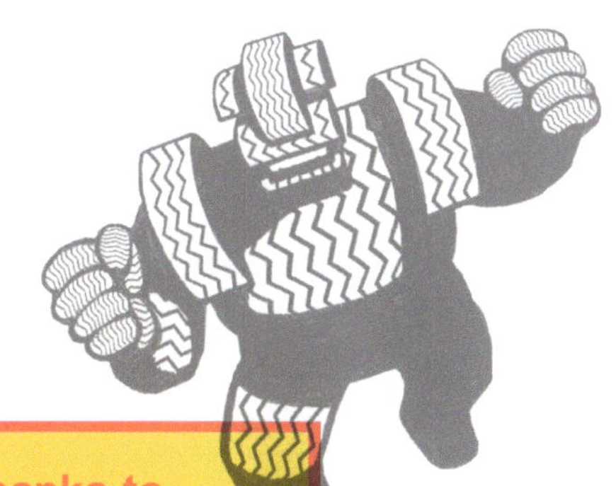

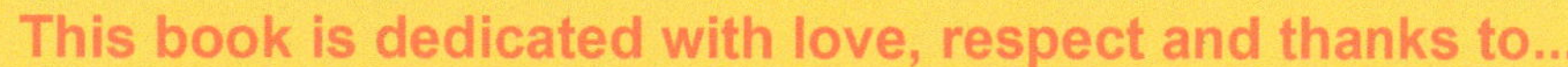

This book is dedicated with love, respect and thanks to...

Curt Swan, George Klein, Carmine Infantino, Murphy Anderson, Gil Kane, Joe Giella, Dick Sprang, Sheldon Moldoff, Joe Kubert, Alex Toth, John Severin, Marie Severin, Gene Colan, Wally Wood, Will Elder, Jack Davis, George Woodbridge, Don Martin, Harvey Kurtzman, Mike Sekowsky, Frank Frazetta, Norman Mingo, Kelly Freas, Reed Crandall, Gray Morrow, Jerry Grandenetti, Fred Rhoads, George Baker, Dave Berg, Al Jaffee, Paul Coker Jr, Neal Adams, Mort Drucker, Angelo Torres, Jack Kirby, Jim Steranko, Steve Ditko Lou Cameron, Robert Webb, David Heames...

some of the artists who made the Silver Age what it was...

and made me want to draw....

And, though he came in on the tail end, to my friend Bernie Wrightson....

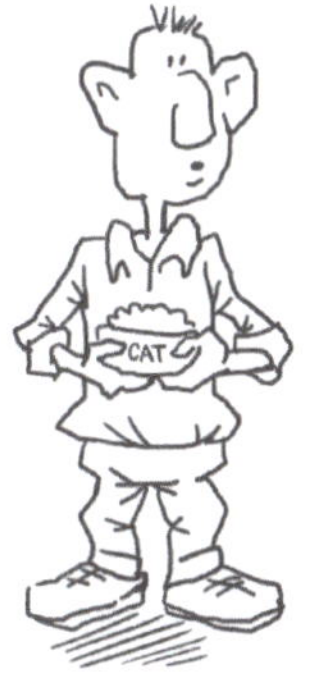

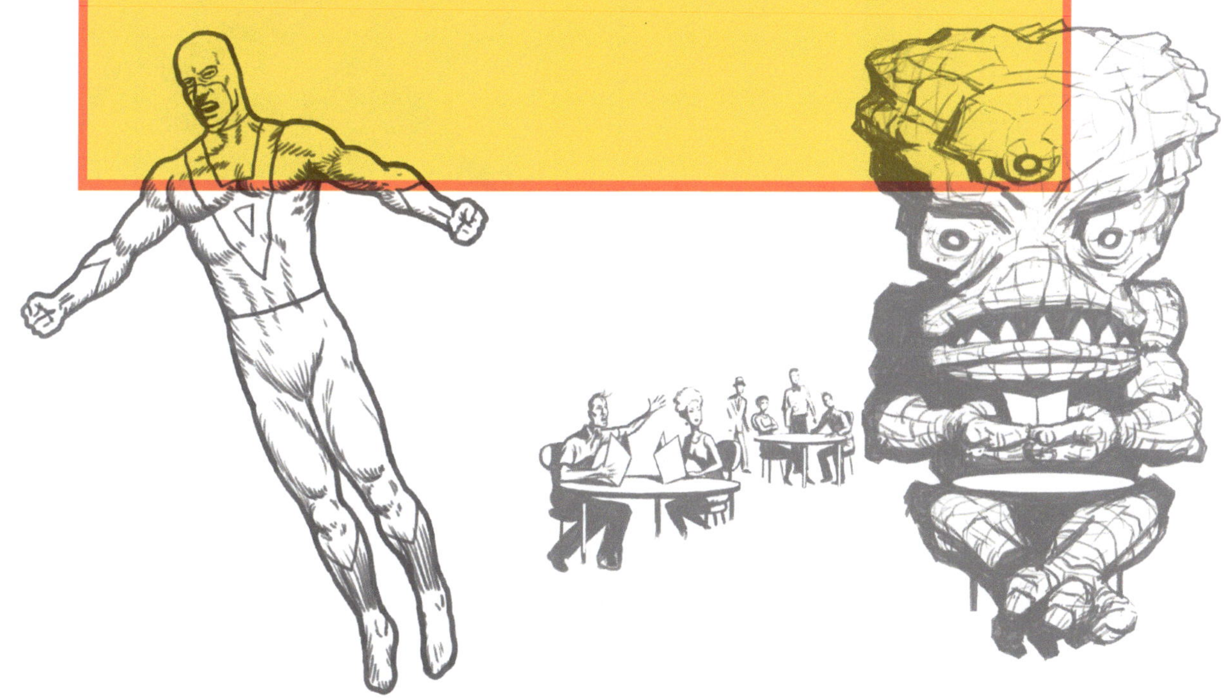

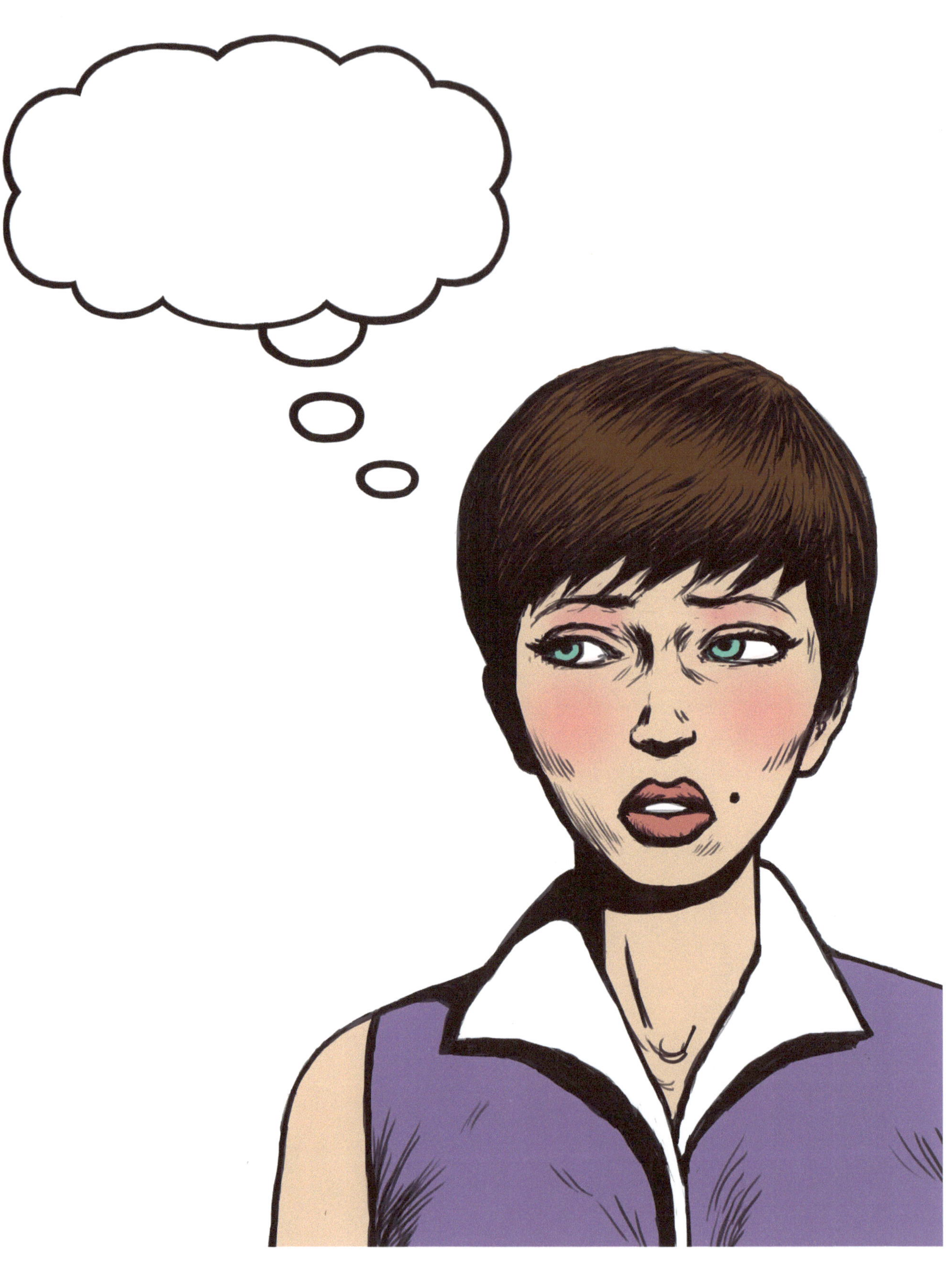

THE LOST COMIC-BOOK COVER-UP
OR; THE FACTS CONCERNING THE RECENT CARNIVAL OF COVERS IN BLAMIREVILLE

I WAS FEELING BLITHE, almost jocund. I put a bowl of food each to our pair of felines, and just then the morning's email arrived.

The first superscription I glanced at was graced with a bemusing faux-comic-book cover that sent a thrill of pleasure through and through me. It was Larry Blamire's; and he was a person I loved and honored most in all the world, outside of my own household.

Though he had not been my boyhood's idol; he had, however, entered the sphere of influences upon my own sensibilities with his antic feature films THE LOST SKELETON OF CADAVRA (2001), TRAIL OF THE SCREAMING FOREHEAD (2007) and THE LOST SKELETON RETURNS AGAIN (2009); and my subsequent maturing, which is fatal to so many enchantments, had not been able to dislodge Blamire's beguiling concoctions from the pedestal they inhabited; no, it had only justified Blamire's right to be there, and placed the dethronement of his works permanently among the impossibilities.

To show how strong his influence over me was and remains, I will observe that long after everybody else's "faux-comic-book covers" had ceased to amuse or affect me in the slightest degree, Blamire's fabrications could still stir my torpid sense of humour into faint signs of life when he put pen to paper—or faux-pen to digital tablet—to fabricate yet another false cover. My childhood love of faked comicbook covers drawn by my next-door neighbor Mitch Casey; my preteen addiction to Mad, Cracked, Sick, and even Tales Calculated to Drive You Bats fake comic book covers; my teenage and college year devotion to National Lampoon's inspired caustic comicbook parodies and their resplendent faux-covers; the work of beloved peers in this sphere, from Batton Lash's Tales of the Unemployed ("Featuring…'The Man Without a Job!'") to Rick Veitch's intoxicating entries for his collaborations with Alan Moore; my own comics career dabblings with such nonsense in projects like 1963 for Image Comics; even Harry Bliss's New Yorker riffs on Jack Kirby Silver Age Timely/Atlas monster comics; all had passed, passed like an elder citizen's gas. All things have their limit, in this world.

A happy day came at last, when even Larry Blamire's faux-comic-book covers could no longer move me. I was not merely glad to see that day arrive; I was more than glad—I was grateful; for when its sun had set, the one alloy that was able to mar my enjoyment of real comic-book covers had at long last evaporated. Prior to that fateful email, I had arrived at the ability to contemplate even Blamire's wildest confections thereafter calmly, peacefully, contentedly indifferent, and remain absolutely, adamantinely indifferent.

Well, the sight of this email with a new Blamire creation reminded me that I was getting very hungry to experience Blamire's work again and anew. I easily guessed what I should find in this email. I opened it. Good! just as I expected; another Blamire faux-cover!

Within nanoseconds, I was undone.

Damn it, I laughed. Damn you, Blamire!

Since that day my life is all bliss. Bliss, unalloyed bliss. Nothing in all the world could persuade me to ever hold in my hands a real comic-book again. I disposed of all my old comic book collection, and began the world anew. I torched thirty-eight long white boxes of rare Golden Age, Pre-Code, and Silver Age genre comicbooks during the first two weeks—all of them on account of the superiority of Blamire's falsehoods. I burned three comic art museum collections as well, though they were neither mine nor even in my home state, because the mere knowledge of their existence threatened my unbesmirched enjoyment of further Blamire creations. I swindled a dealer and some elderly collectors out of their last vintage comics, which were indeed rare ones, though not in absolute mint condition, I believe, only to put those to the torch as well. I have also committed scores of crimes, of various kinds, all to destroy all evidence of comic books past and present, and have enjoyed my work exceedingly, whereas it would formerly have broken my heart and turned my gray hair to silver, I have no doubt.

In conclusion I wish to state, by way of advertisement, that any fool desiring assorted slabbed Golden Age and Silver Age rarities that have been melted into a 2001-like monolith, whether for artistic or scientific purposes, will do well to examine the flame-scorched slab in my cellar before purchasing elsewhere, as these slabbed comic rarities were all selected and prepared by myself to be turned into one black-plastic monstrosity, and can be had at a low rate, because I wish to clear out my basement and get ready for the a New Year's worth of atrocities against aging paper blemished by the once-beloved archaic four-color printing of yore.

- Stephen R. Bissette, The Mountains of Madness, Summer/Fall 2018
[With all due apologies to Samuel Clemens/Mark Twain]

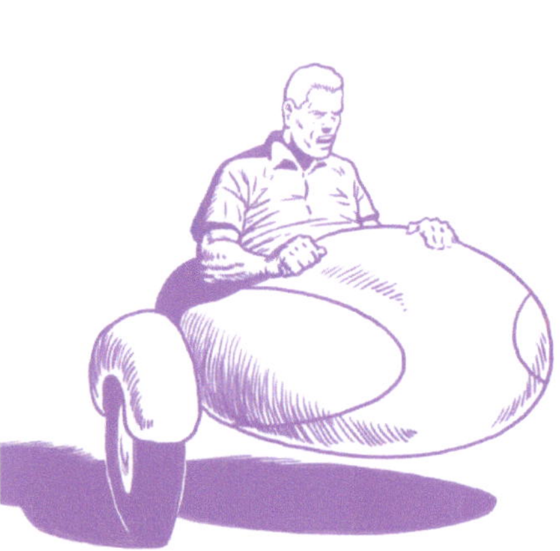

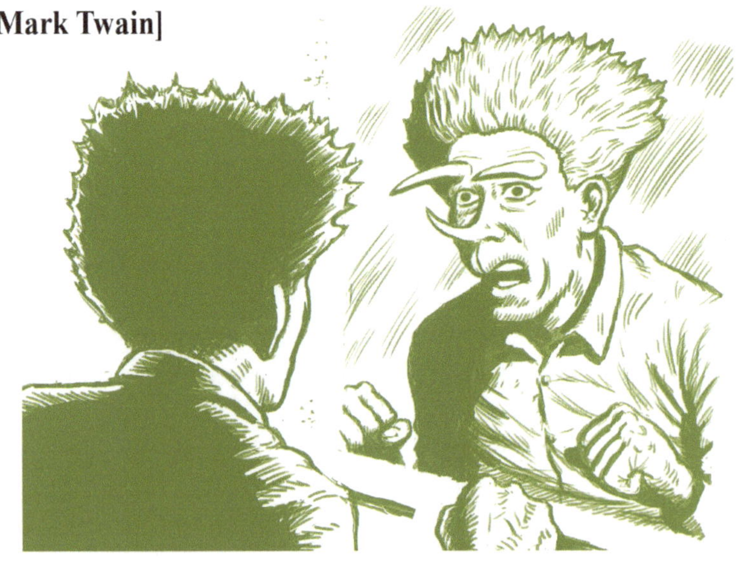

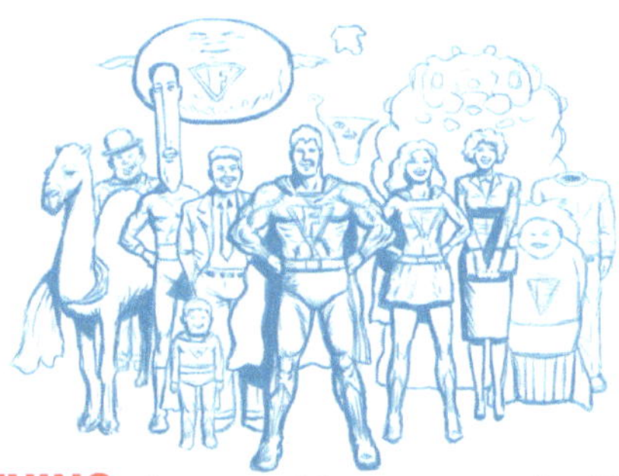

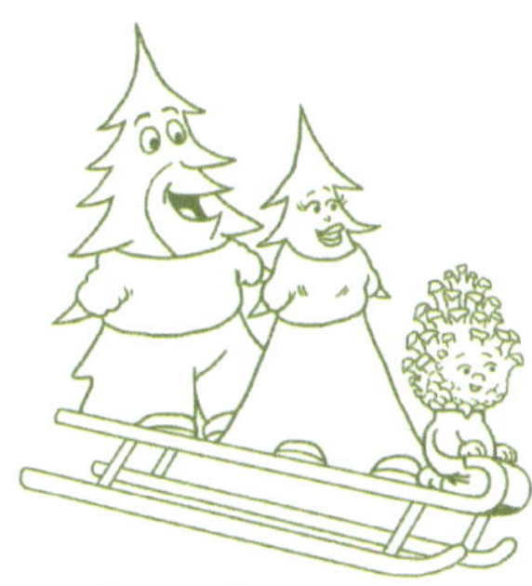

THERE'S SOMETHING about a 12-cent comic. Nostalgia, of course, since they were my first discoveries on the magical spinner rack. And pureness of entertainment. They were fun.

I'm no historian, but that might have been the last time comics were aimed strictly at kids. This period of comic books, mid-60's to 1970, is dubbed "The Silver Age." As a DC kid (didn't catch up with Marvel till adulthood) it seemed to me that their "new look" was the first sign of looming adultification.

I miss those comics and, as the parent of a seven-year-old, I find myself wishing they'd make a return. In fact I occasionally score "reader copies" for him. These things are packed with superb art and storytelling; the best of surviving Golden Age creators, combined with exciting up-and-comers. I don't think this deep creative well has ever been matched.

The comic logo I made up says "clean comics," but it doesn't refer to moral judgement or personal hygiene but rather the crisp clear look of the time. Clean lines and compositions, layouts that invite the eye rather than confuse it with self-conscious busyness. Storytelling.

My favorite artist team was Curt Swan on pencils, inked by George Klein. Ironically, I've heard them referred to as "safe" or "standard," towing the company line. I think their illustrating was a thing of beauty. Of DC regulars, those two, plus Carmine Infantino and Murphy Anderson, probably had the most influence on me (my dedication lists others).

And to love Silver Age DC is to also embrace, yes, the sheer high strangeness of the Jack Schiff Batman years when Dark Knight was more Daft Knight. Dick Sprang is my favorite artist of those, but I also love the awkward innocence of Sheldon Moldoff. Think what you will, these wild flights of anything-can-happen fancy took a kid places. Odd places, from which I never returned. Instead of looking *real,* they happily embraced *anti-real.* Perhaps my first taste of surrealism.

When I created my *Strange Popcorn Ceiling Tales* cover on a whim (just gettin' my kicks) it was inspired by that wonderful comic book conceit: the expositional exclamation. Often beginning with a spirited "Great Scott!" these outbursts told us exactly what was happening. My favorite is the Overly Helpful Bystander, usually some guy in suit and tie, probably on his way to or from work, who stops to blurt out what's happening, for our benefit, at great risk to life and limb. Who thinks of that in the thick of things? While about to be eaten?

As soon as I finished that gag cover I was off and running, churning them out like it was some sick, twisted, but lovable, addiction. It was really fun in an obsessive way.

I wanted to riff all types: DC, Marvel, Dell/Gold Key, Harvey, Charlton, ACG, superhero, horror, science fiction, humor, western. But they needed to pass muster, or at least ketchup. It was vital they look real. Sorta. Kinda. Covers from an alternate reality.

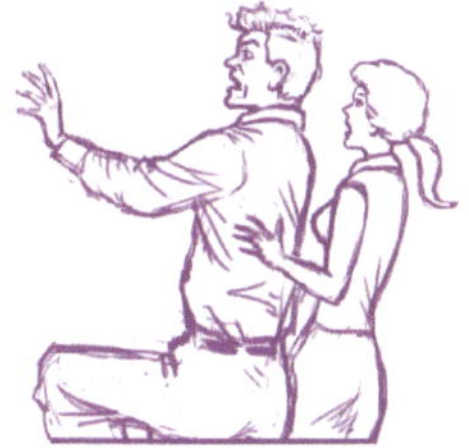

Who was I kidding? This was not your simple garden variety spoofery (the kind Mom used to make). As ideas continued to storm my brain, it became apparent through their increasing strangeness that these faux covers were merely an excuse to visit two of my favorite relatives: Cousin Absurdity and Uncle Surrealism. I hadn't painted in a while, and it was obvious even to the most neglected homing squash that the covers had become my vehicle du jour (literally "ostrich of the minute") for expressing those things too silly to not be expressed. My gosh you are lucky.

I cannot overstate the importance of variety. Variety is the engine that drives my striped tie. Maybe it's my unnatural resistance to being labelled or pinned down, but I really wanted it to look like several artists did this. At gunpoint. With some humor titles, I was able to employ my own sketchy cartoon style, which I call "sketchy." Other times I'd glance at some Harveys and try to match the house look. Or the unusually subdued palette of Marvel westerns. For superheroes, SF and horror, I used pretty much my own style, and you might see some Swan-Klein-Infantino-Anderson influence (I should be so lucky). Sometimes I would work up sketches rather than "inking" over in a separate layer (these are digital, on Wacom Tablet). It added diversity and, if I'm not mistaken, a hint of pecan.

But the Kirby experience.... I had to include Jack Kirby style monsters or not call myself a known haberdasher. Though I'd seen them before, I pored through covers, and it seemed like this time I was really *seeing* them. When I started drawing, a strange thing happened. I had decided to suggest Kirby's unique monsters in my own style. But when I tried to use my typical shading lines, it just wasn't working. Back up, erase, repeat. Soon I was carried away, using massive blocks and jagged freeform lines to suggest mass. I let my instincts take over and lost track of time. It happened on each of my three Kirby monster covers. Now, I will not be so arrogant as to suggest that the King guided my hand. But I was certainly under his influence. And suddenly... I loved Jack Kirby.

Early in this process, I created a system, a template with logos and such that I could just plug into. First I made the heading, which for me set the tone of the whole piece. In many cases I sought to match specific fonts to riff familiar titles. This was laborious and may sound boring, but it became one of my favorite things. I was like a gleeful counterfeiter in a basement who couldn't wait to not make money. I found that the title set the tone for the whole piece. Every now and then I felt the exaltation of completing what I dubbed *My Stupidest Yet.* I wondered if it would ever be topped. It usually was.

Eventually, my covers reflected actual comics less and less, and by the time I got to *The Sounds of the Circus* I was pretty much off the deep end.

This was a really odd project. I never set out to do it, never "thought it up." It just happened. I mean, you almost didn't have this.

Now I'm wondering what your life would be without this book and it scares me, it just scares me so much.

- Larry Blamire

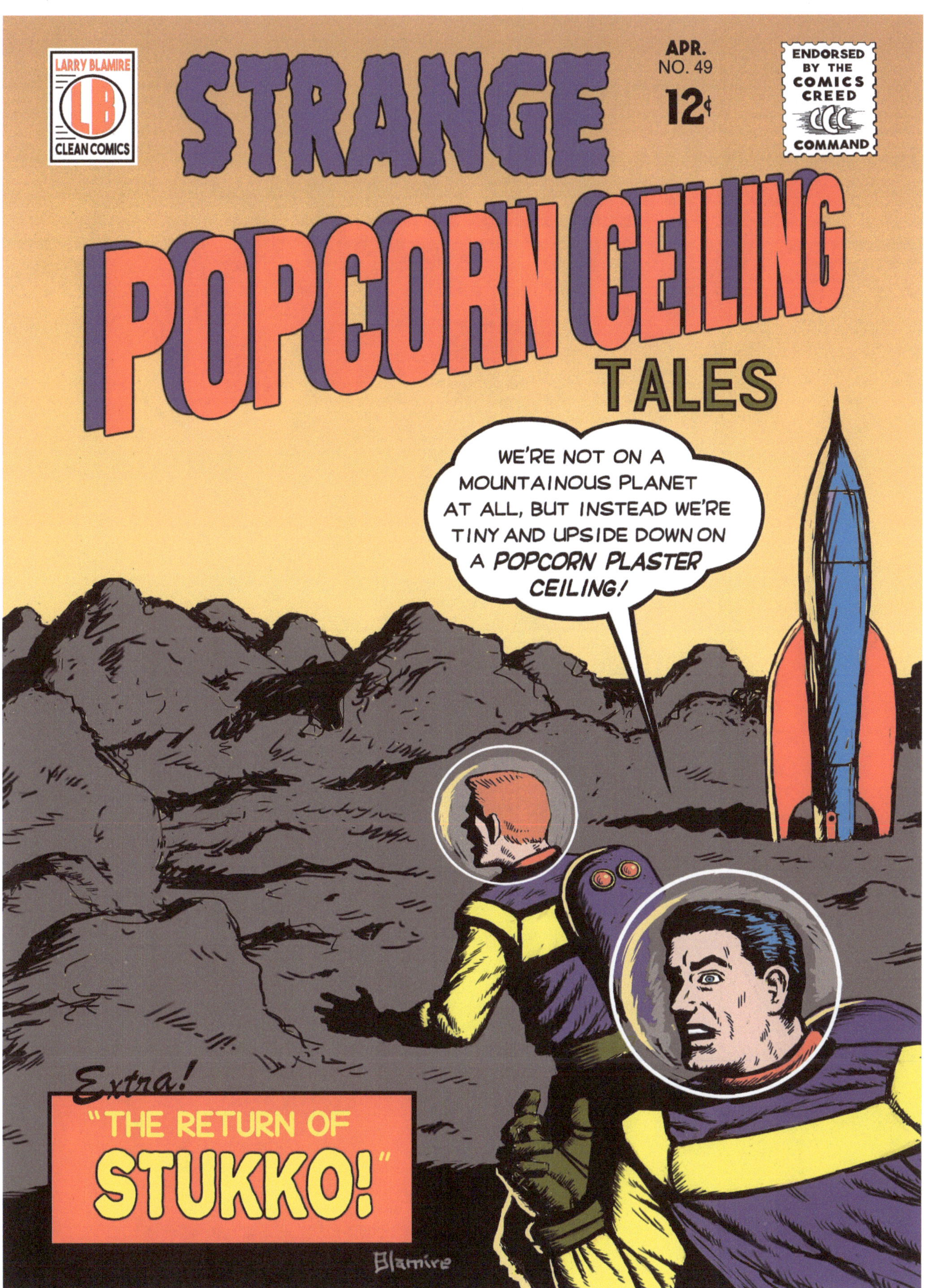
LARRY BLAMIRE
LB
CLEAN COMICS
STRANGE
APR.
NO. 49
12¢
ENDORSED BY THE COMICS CREED
CCC
COMMAND
POPCORN CEILING
TALES
WE'RE NOT ON A MOUNTAINOUS PLANET AT ALL, BUT INSTEAD WE'RE TINY AND UPSIDE DOWN ON A *POPCORN PLASTER CEILING!*
Extra!
"THE RETURN OF STUKKO!"
Blamire

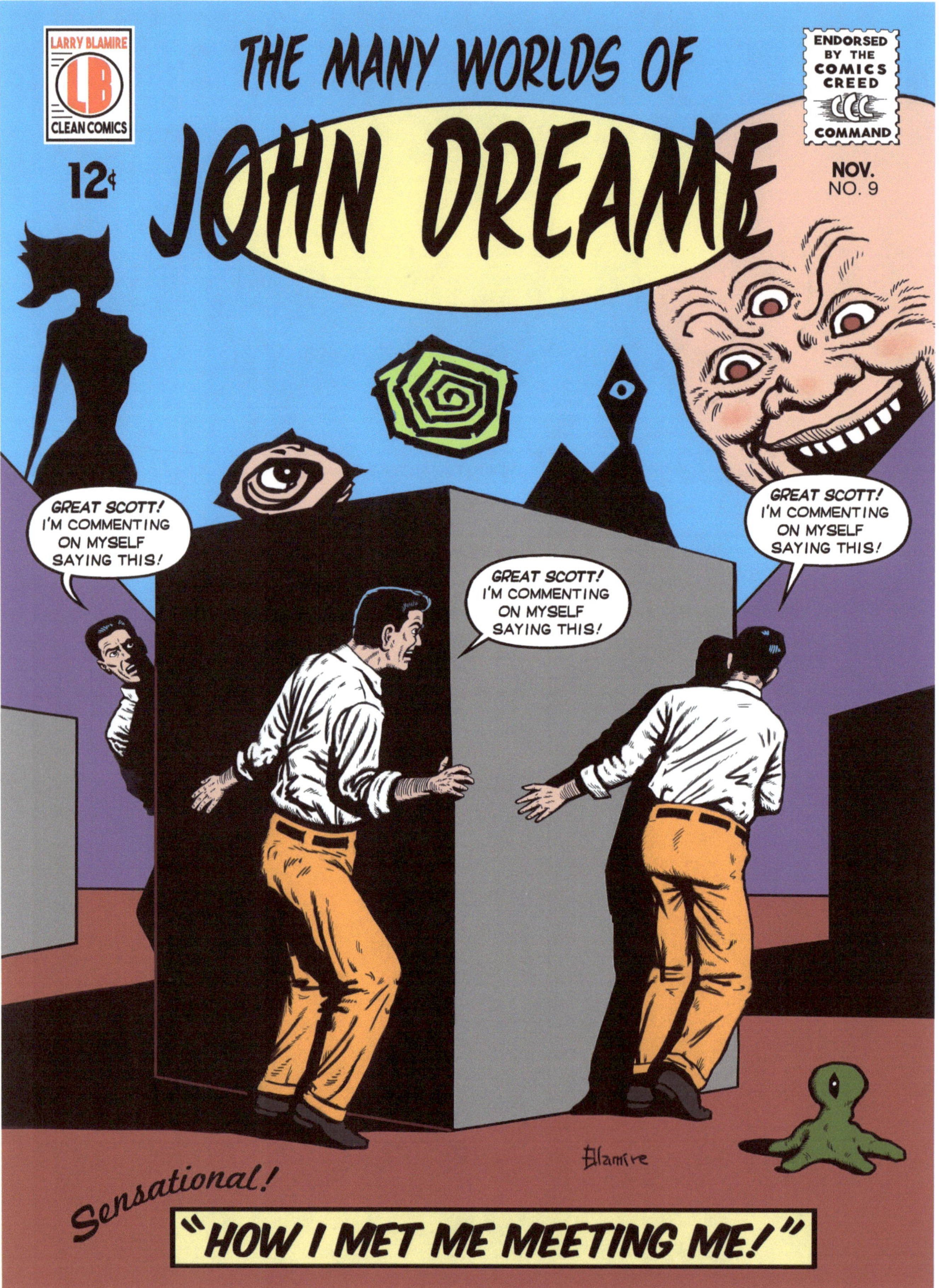
LARRY BLAMIRE
LB
CLEAN COMICS
12¢
THE MANY WORLDS OF
JOHN DREAME
ENDORSED BY THE COMICS CREED
CCC
COMMAND
NOV.
NO. 9
GREAT SCOTT! I'M COMMENTING ON MYSELF SAYING THIS!
GREAT SCOTT! I'M COMMENTING ON MYSELF SAYING THIS!
GREAT SCOTT! I'M COMMENTING ON MYSELF SAYING THIS!
Blamire
Sensational!
"HOW I MET ME MEETING ME!"

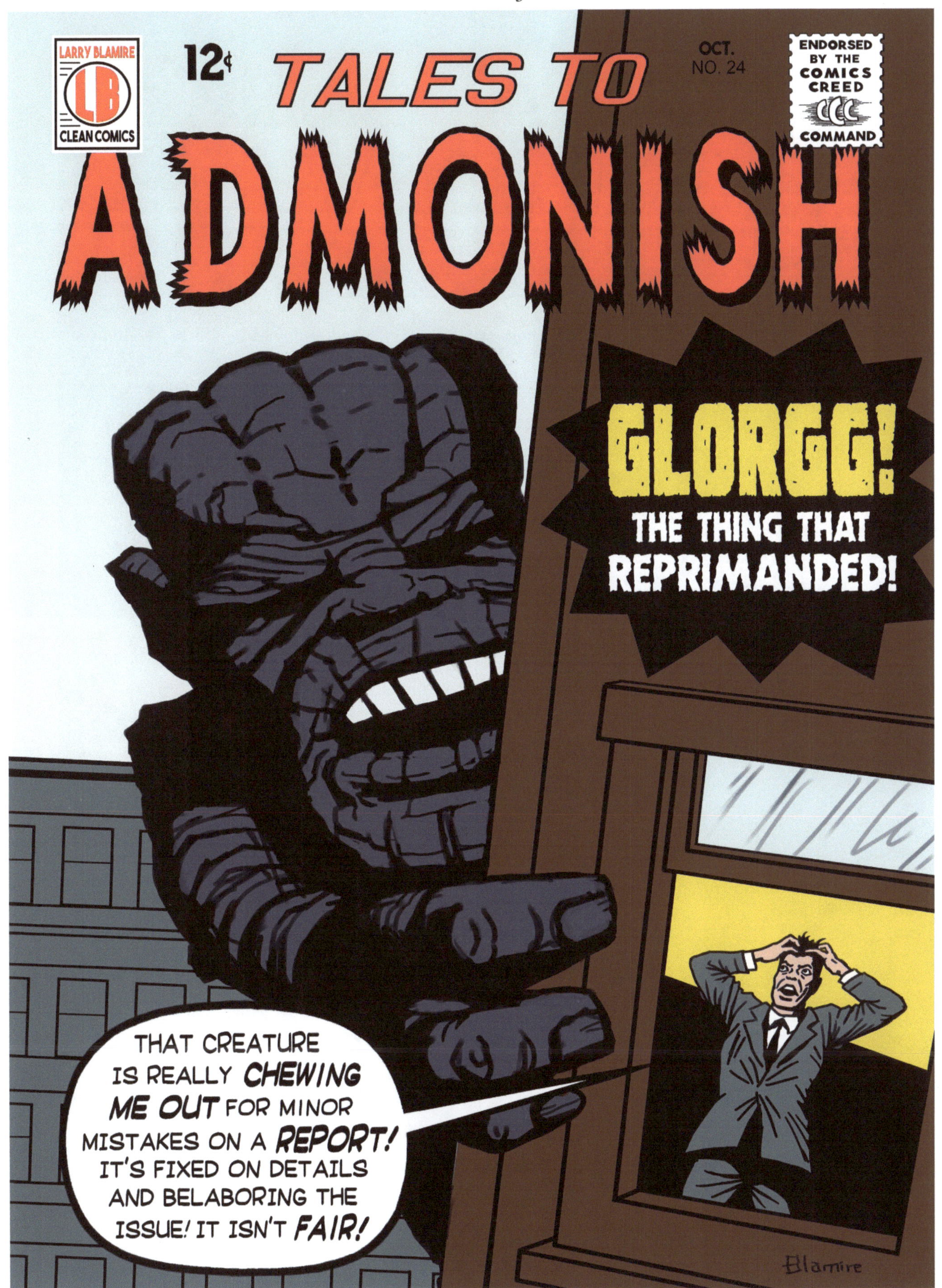
LARRY BLAMIRE
LB
CLEAN COMICS
12¢
TALES TO
ADMONISH
OCT.
NO. 24
ENDORSED BY THE COMICS CREED
CCC
COMMAND
GLORGG!
THE THING THAT REPRIMANDED!
THAT CREATURE IS REALLY CHEWING ME OUT FOR MINOR MISTAKES ON A REPORT! IT'S FIXED ON DETAILS AND BELABORING THE ISSUE! IT ISN'T FAIR!
Blamire

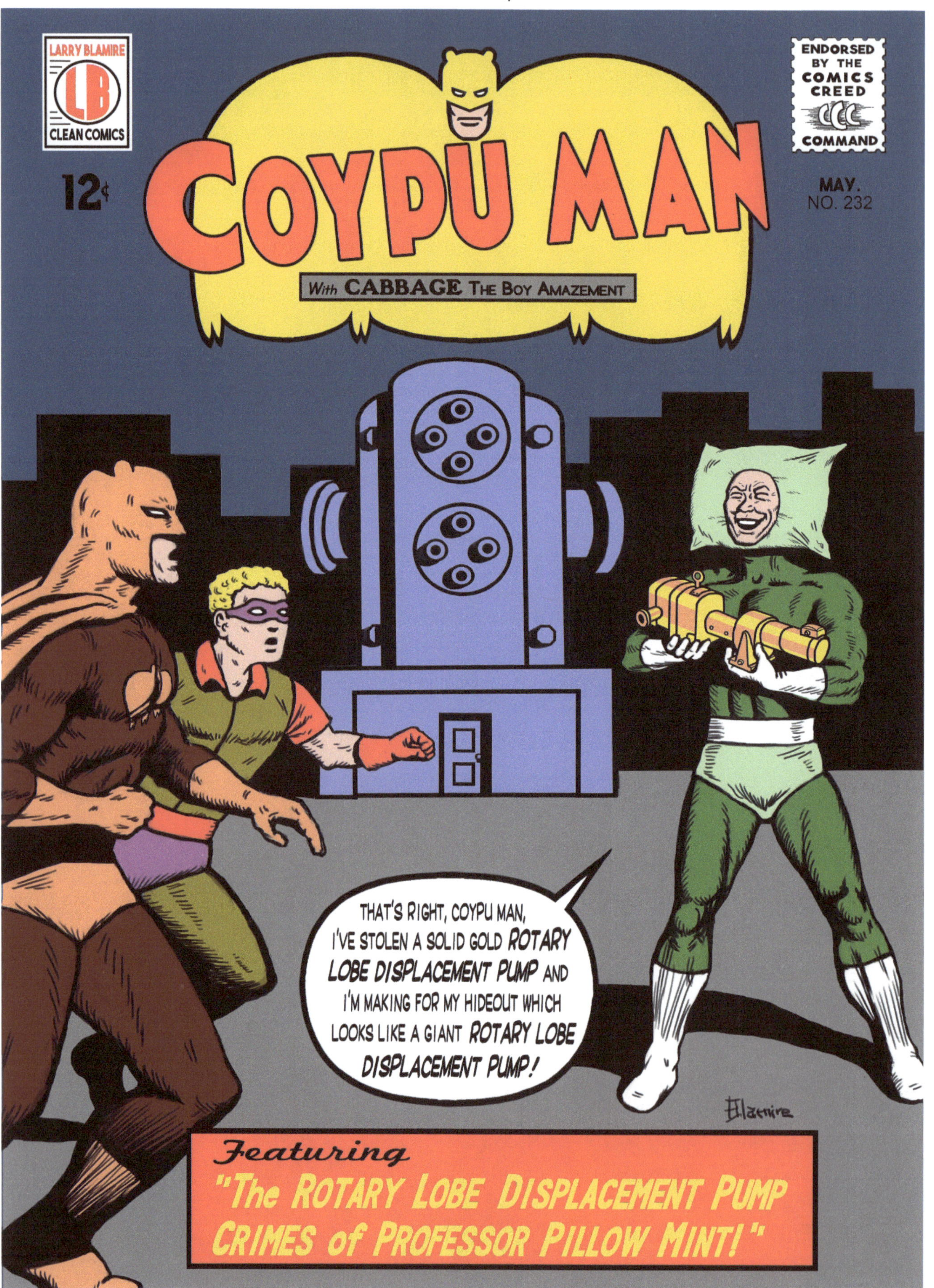
LARRY BLAMIRE
LB
CLEAN COMICS
ENDORSED BY THE COMICS CREED COMMAND
CCC
12¢
COYPU MAN
MAY.
NO. 232
With CABBAGE The Boy Amazement
THAT'S RIGHT, COYPU MAN, I'VE STOLEN A SOLID GOLD ROTARY LOBE DISPLACEMENT PUMP AND I'M MAKING FOR MY HIDEOUT WHICH LOOKS LIKE A GIANT ROTARY LOBE DISPLACEMENT PUMP!
Blamire
Featuring
"The ROTARY LOBE DISPLACEMENT PUMP CRIMES of PROFESSOR PILLOW MINT!"

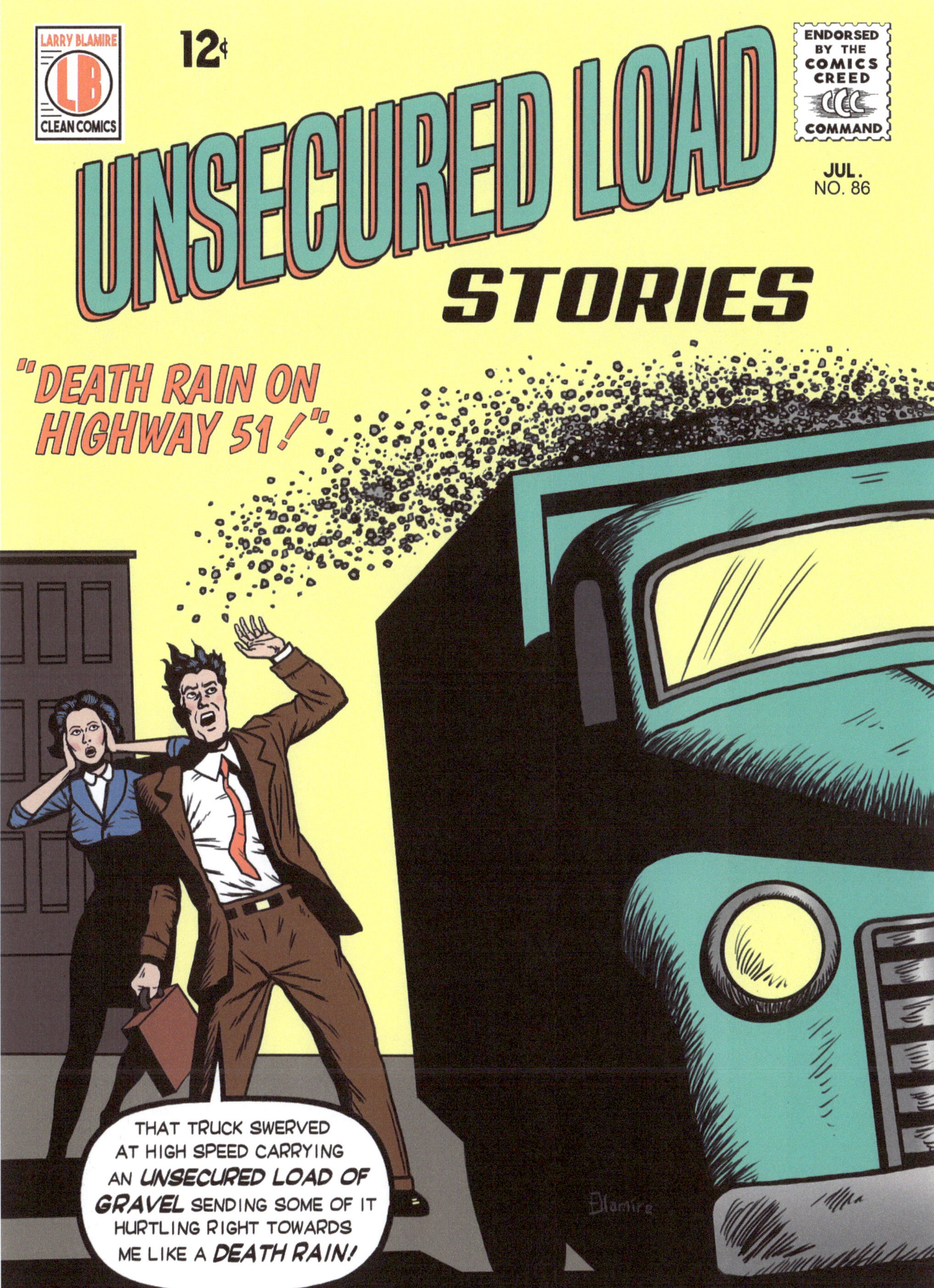
LARRY BLAMIRE
LB
CLEAN COMICS
12¢
UNSECURED LOAD
STORIES
ENDORSED BY THE COMICS CREED
CCC
COMMAND
JUL.
NO. 86
"DEATH RAIN ON HIGHWAY 51!"
THAT TRUCK SWERVED AT HIGH SPEED CARRYING AN UNSECURED LOAD OF GRAVEL SENDING SOME OF IT HURTLING RIGHT TOWARDS ME LIKE A DEATH RAIN!
Blamire

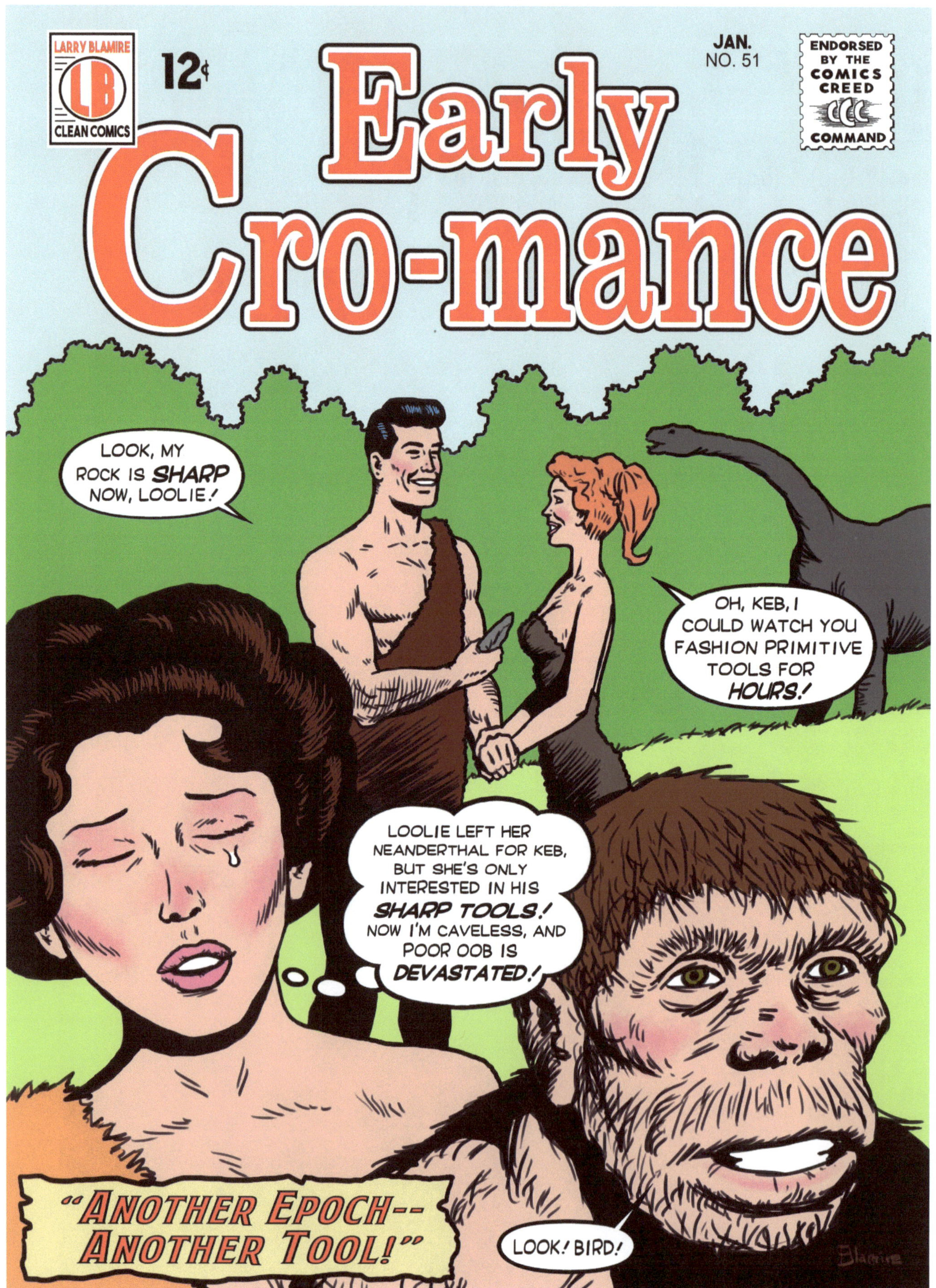
LARRY BLAMIRE
LB
CLEAN COMICS
12¢
Early Cro-mance
JAN.
NO. 51
ENDORSED BY THE COMICS CREED
CCC
COMMAND
LOOK, MY ROCK IS SHARP NOW, LOOLIE!
OH, KEB, I COULD WATCH YOU FASHION PRIMITIVE TOOLS FOR HOURS!
LOOLIE LEFT HER NEANDERTHAL FOR KEB, BUT SHE'S ONLY INTERESTED IN HIS SHARP TOOLS! NOW I'M CAVELESS, AND POOR OOB IS DEVASTATED!
"ANOTHER EPOCH-- ANOTHER TOOL!"
LOOK! BIRD!
Blamire

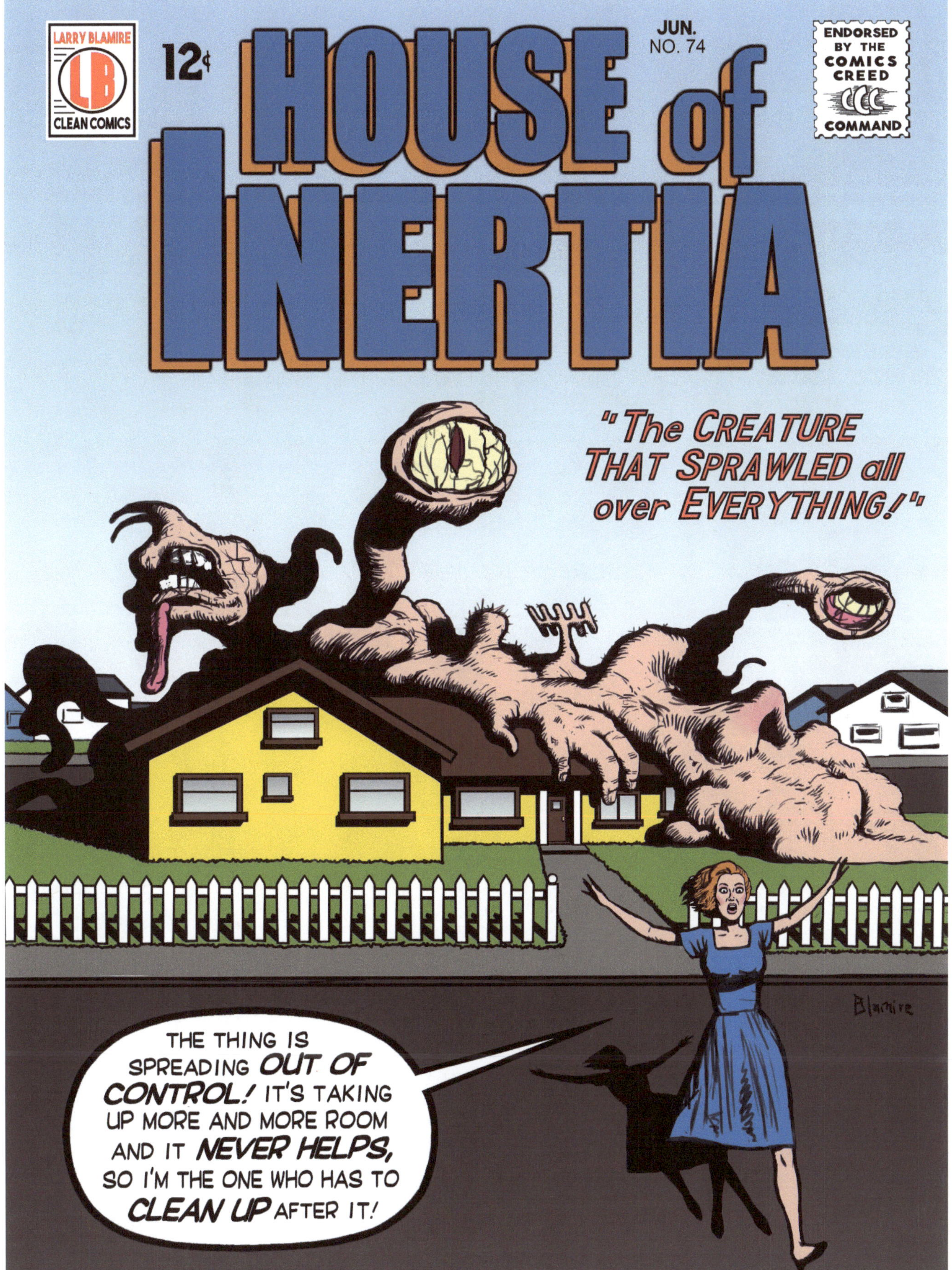
LARRY BLAMIRE
LB
CLEAN COMICS
12¢
HOUSE of INERTIA
JUN.
NO. 74
ENDORSED BY THE COMICS CREED
CCC
COMMAND
"The CREATURE THAT SPRAWLED all over EVERYTHING!"
Blamire
THE THING IS SPREADING OUT OF CONTROL! IT'S TAKING UP MORE AND MORE ROOM AND IT NEVER HELPS, SO I'M THE ONE WHO HAS TO CLEAN UP AFTER IT!

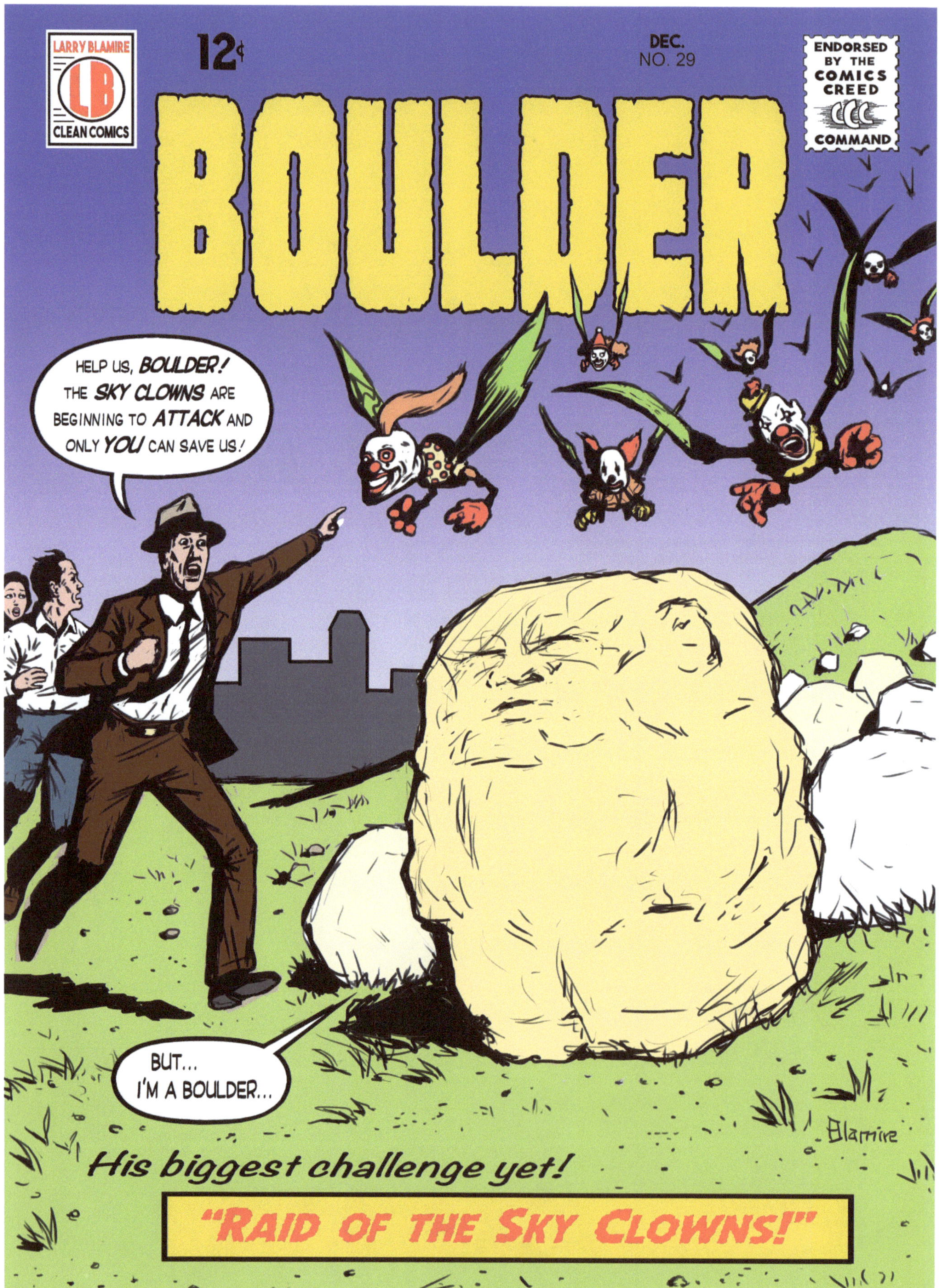
LARRY BLAMIRE
LB
CLEAN COMICS
12¢
DEC.
NO. 29
ENDORSED BY THE COMICS CREED
CCC
COMMAND
BOULDER
HELP US, BOULDER! THE SKY CLOWNS ARE BEGINNING TO ATTACK AND ONLY YOU CAN SAVE US!
BUT... I'M A BOULDER...
Blamire
His biggest challenge yet!
"RAID OF THE SKY CLOWNS!"

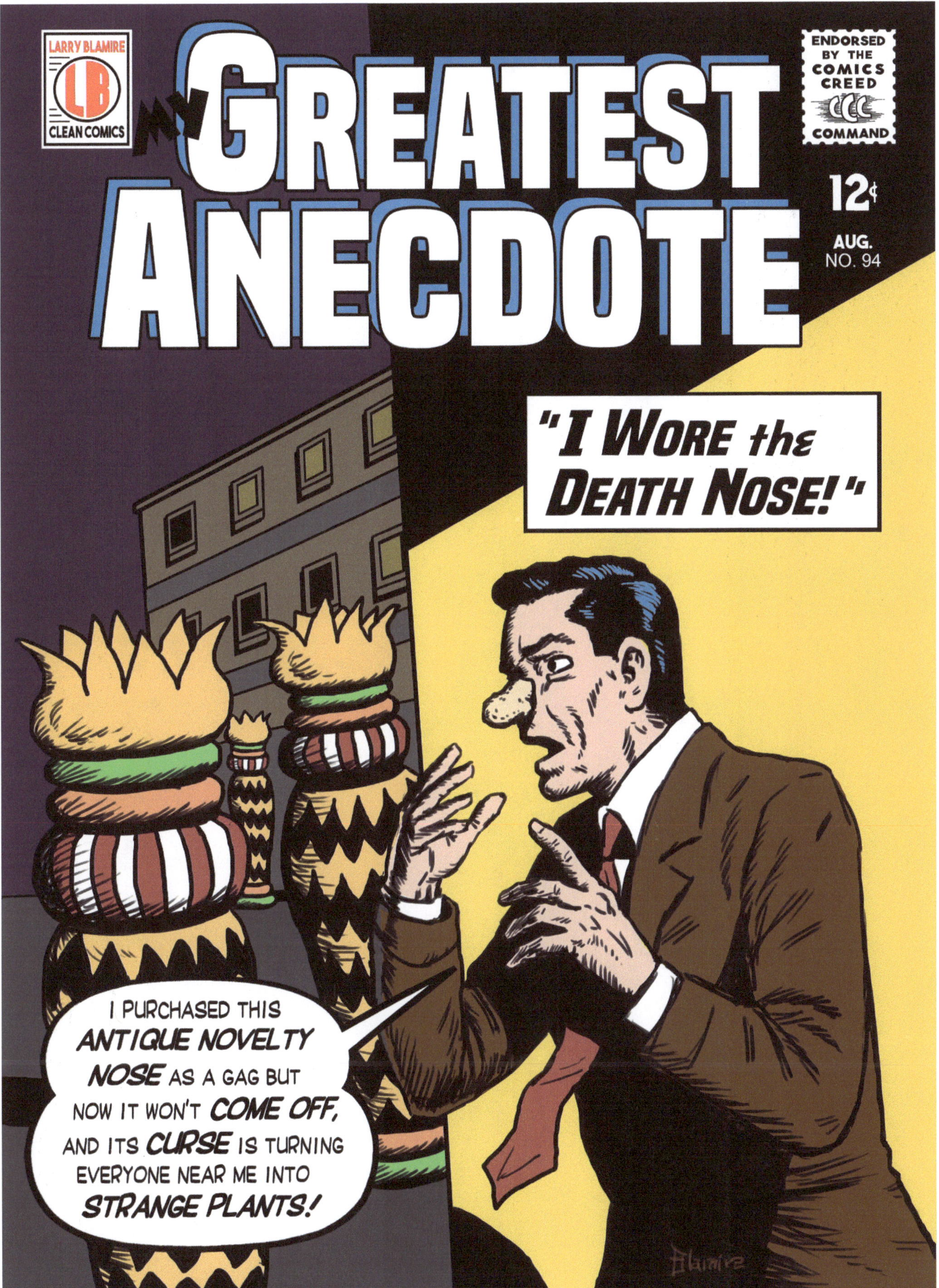

LARRY BLAMIRE
LB
CLEAN COMICS
MY GREATEST ANECDOTE
ENDORSED BY THE COMICS CREED
CCC
COMMAND
12¢
AUG.
NO. 94
"I WORE the DEATH NOSE!"
I PURCHASED THIS ANTIQUE NOVELTY NOSE AS A GAG BUT NOW IT WON'T COME OFF, AND ITS CURSE IS TURNING EVERYONE NEAR ME INTO STRANGE PLANTS!
Blamire

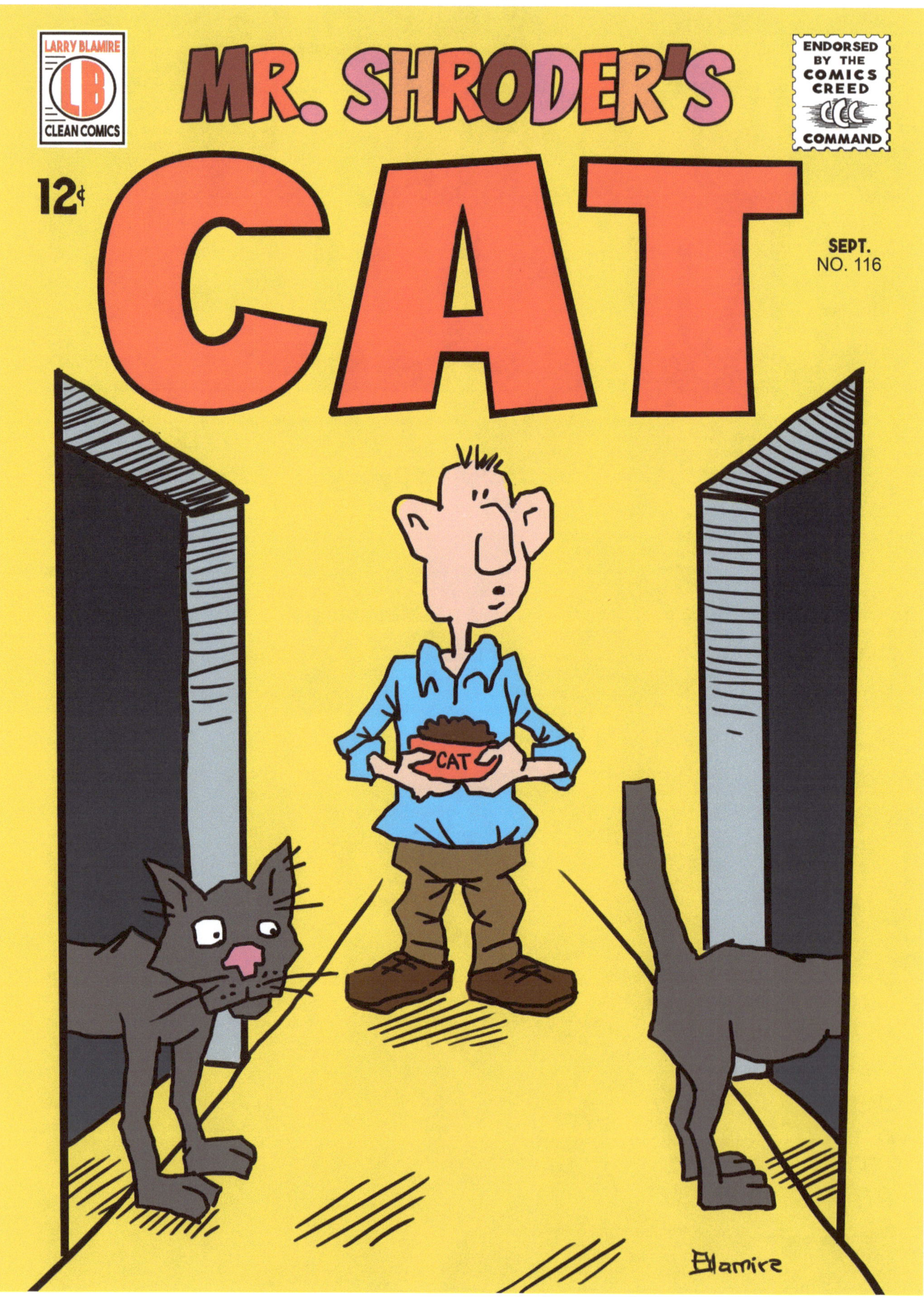
LARRY BLAMIRE
LB
CLEAN COMICS
MR. SHRODER'S
ENDORSED BY THE COMICS CREED
CCC
COMMAND
12¢
CAT
SEPT.
NO. 116
CAT
Blamire

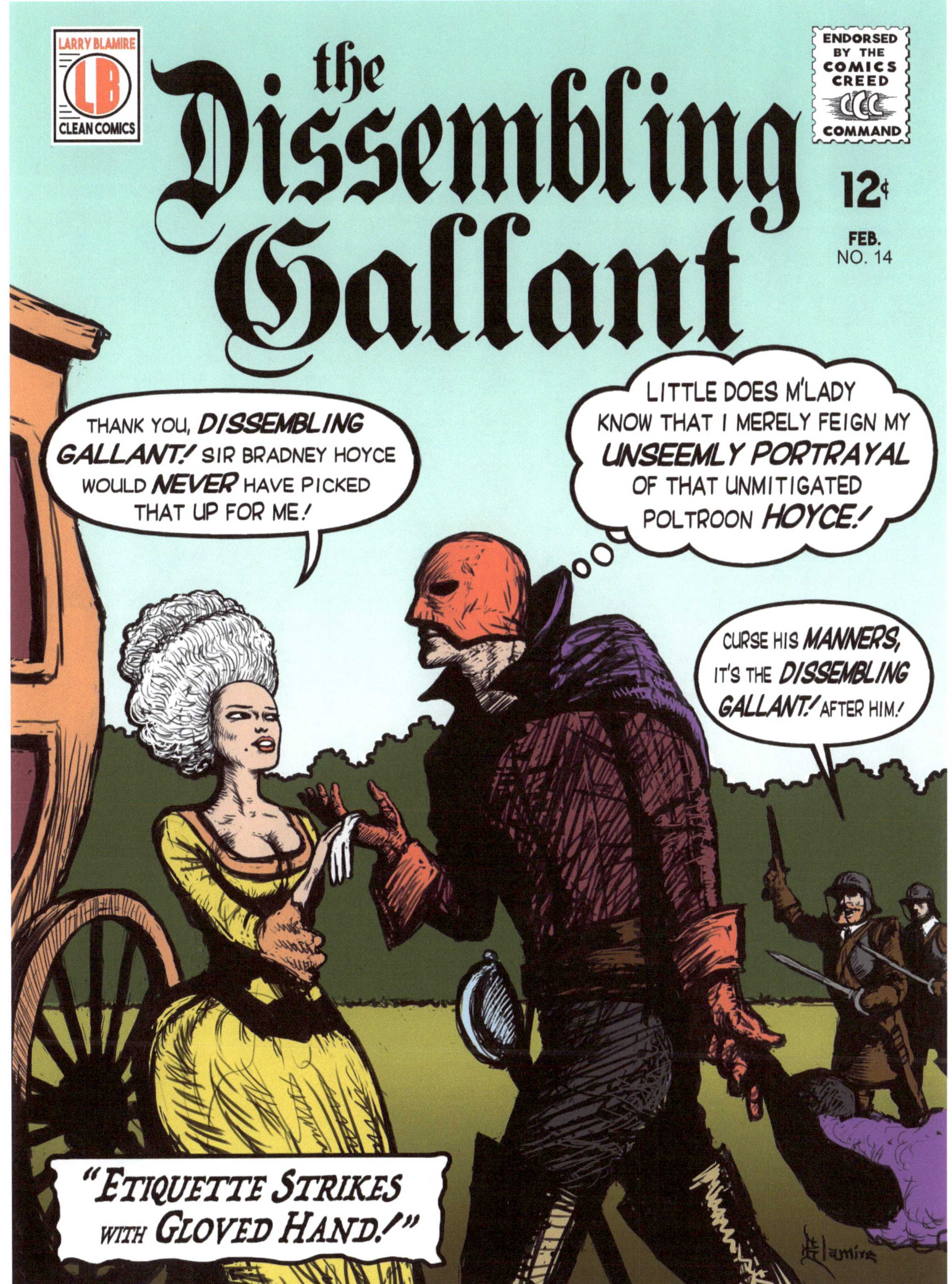
LARRY BLAMIRE
LB
CLEAN COMICS
the Dissembling Gallant
ENDORSED BY THE COMICS CREED
CCC
COMMAND
12¢
FEB.
NO. 14
THANK YOU, DISSEMBLING GALLANT! SIR BRADNEY HOYCE WOULD NEVER HAVE PICKED THAT UP FOR ME!
LITTLE DOES M'LADY KNOW THAT I MERELY FEIGN MY UNSEEMLY PORTRAYAL OF THAT UNMITIGATED POLTROON HOYCE!
CURSE HIS MANNERS, IT'S THE DISSEMBLING GALLANT! AFTER HIM!
"ETIQUETTE STRIKES WITH GLOVED HAND!"
Blamire

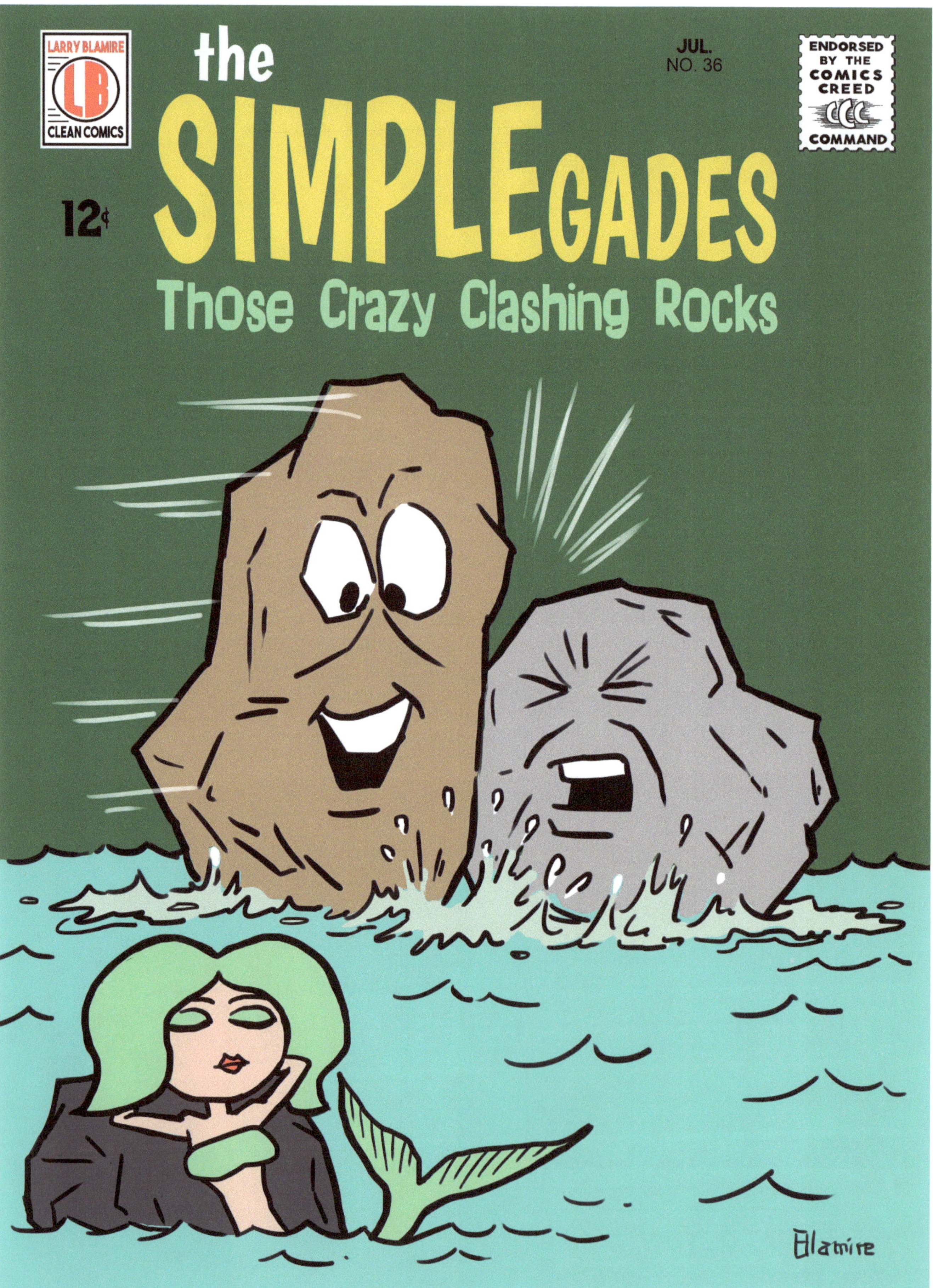
LARRY BLAMIRE
LB
CLEAN COMICS
the
JUL.
NO. 36
ENDORSED BY THE COMICS CREED
CCC
COMMAND
12¢
SIMPLEGADES
Those Crazy Clashing Rocks
Blamire

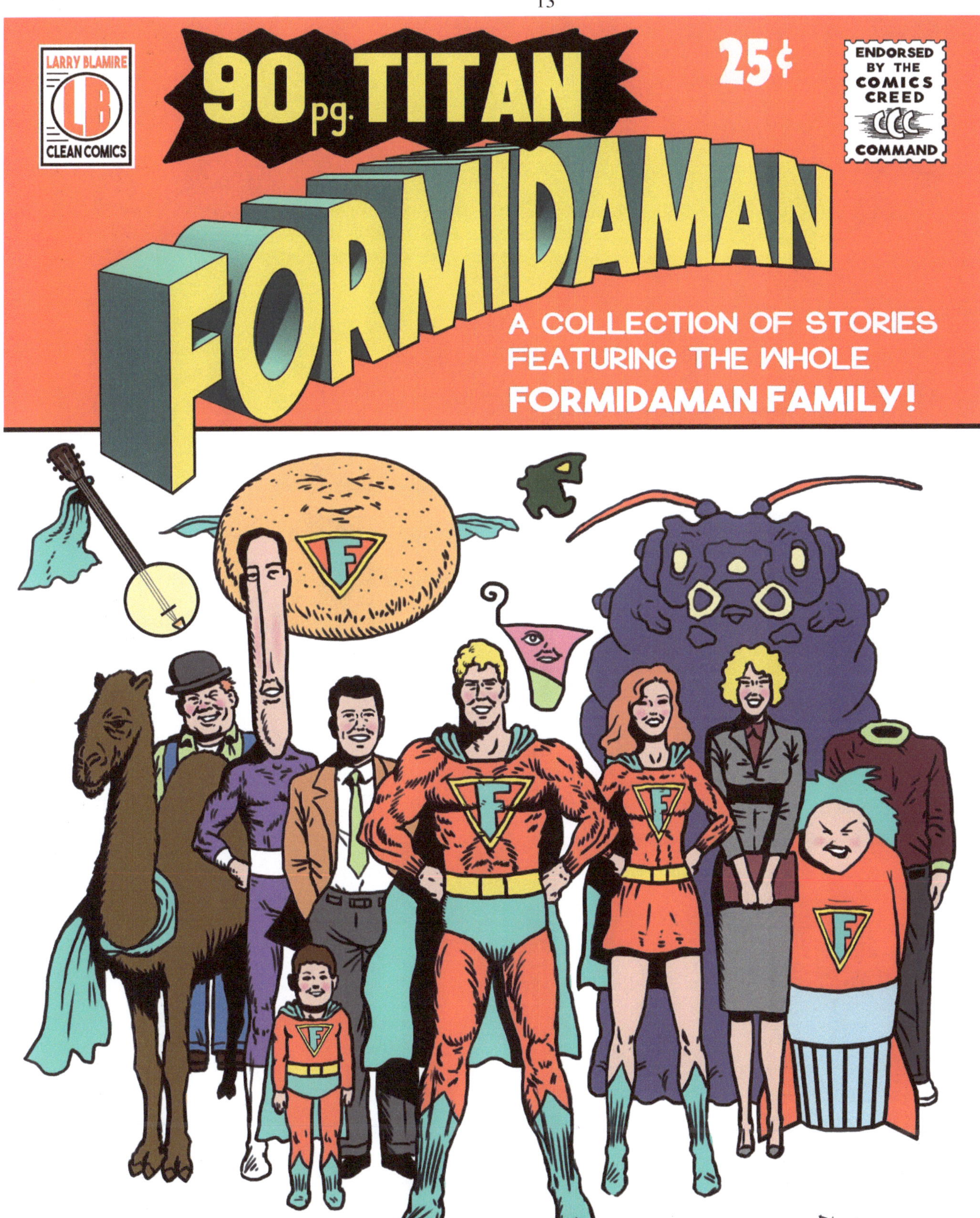

FORMIDAMAN! FORMIDAGIRL! FORMIDATODDLER! FEDDY MEETERS! SUE BLENN! FORMIDACAMEL! VOOS! MR. ACALCUPLEZE! FORMIDACOOKIE! TIMPECK! OBOPOD! FORMIDABANJO! DR. LAWP! KANGOO! ELPY!

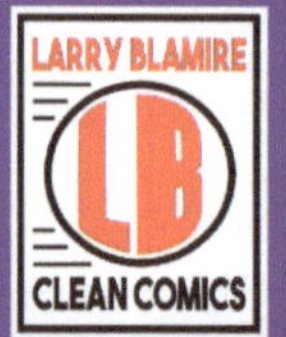

Little Isotope

JAN.
NO. 87

12¢

ENDORSED BY THE COMICS CREED
CCC
COMMAND

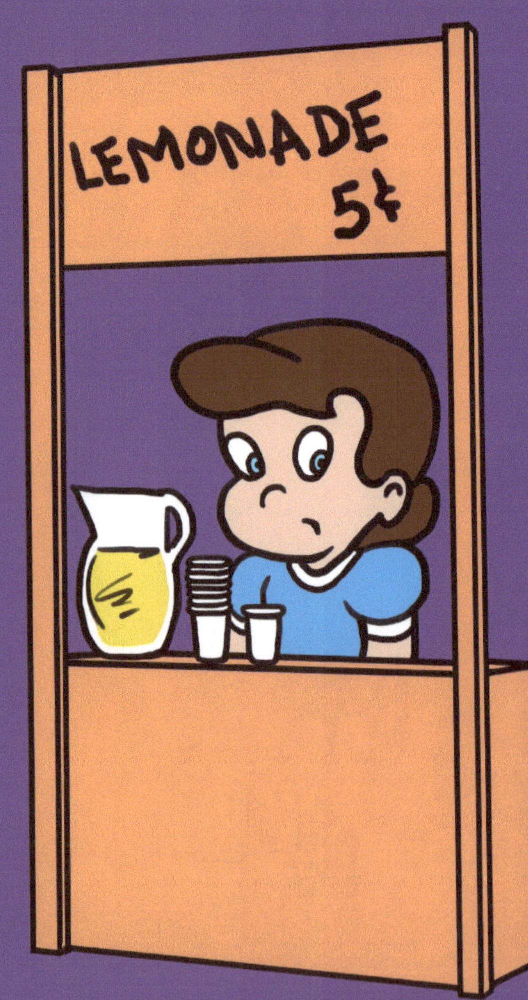

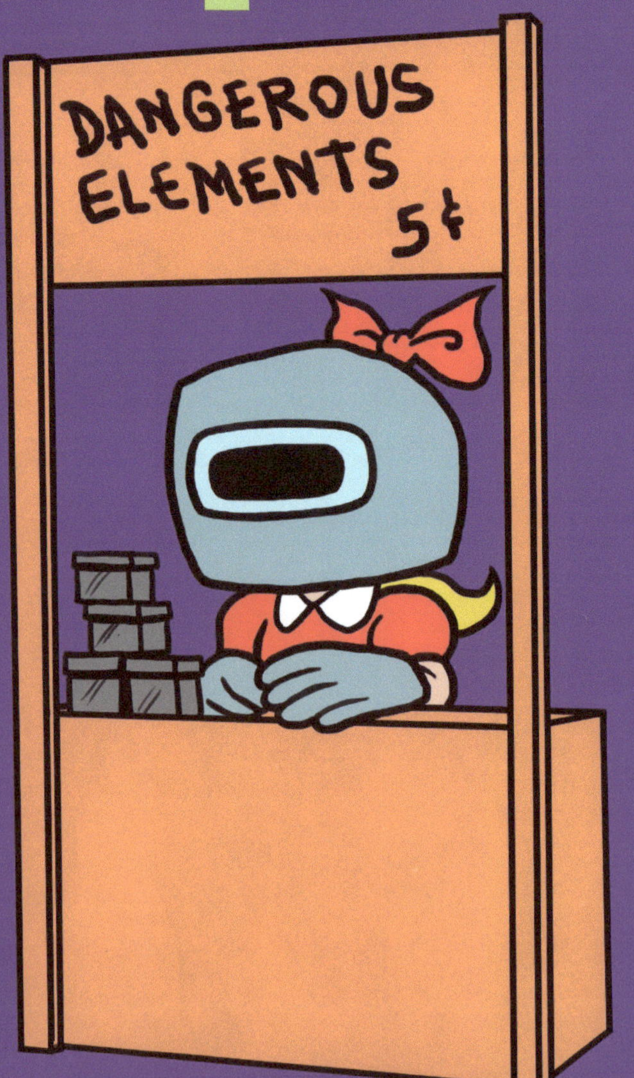

Blamire

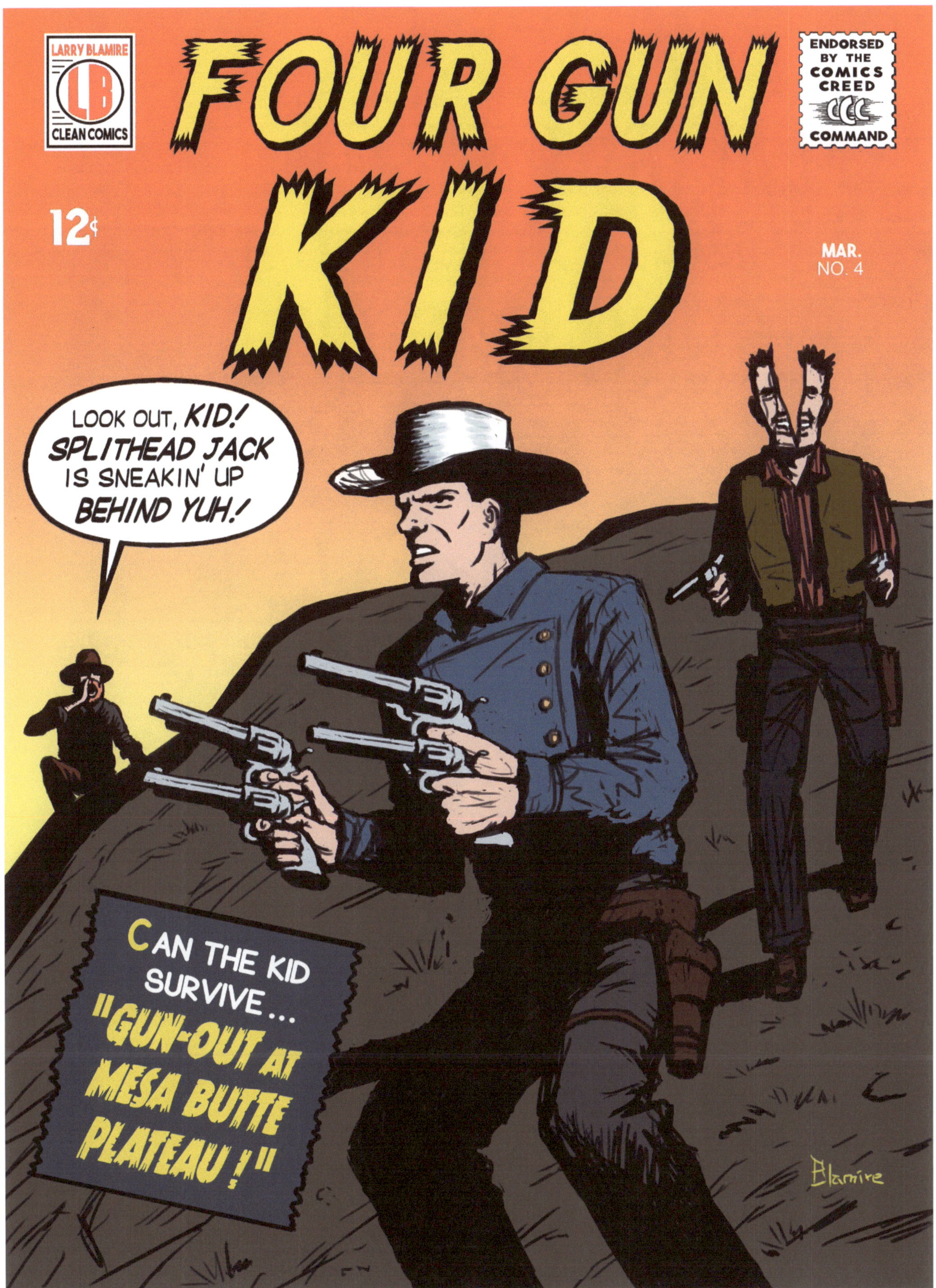
LARRY BLAMIRE
LB
CLEAN COMICS
FOUR GUN KID
ENDORSED BY THE COMICS CREED
CCCC
COMMAND
12¢
MAR.
NO. 4
LOOK OUT, KID! SPLITHEAD JACK IS SNEAKIN' UP BEHIND YUH!
CAN THE KID SURVIVE... "GUN-OUT AT MESA BUTTE PLATEAU!"
Blamire

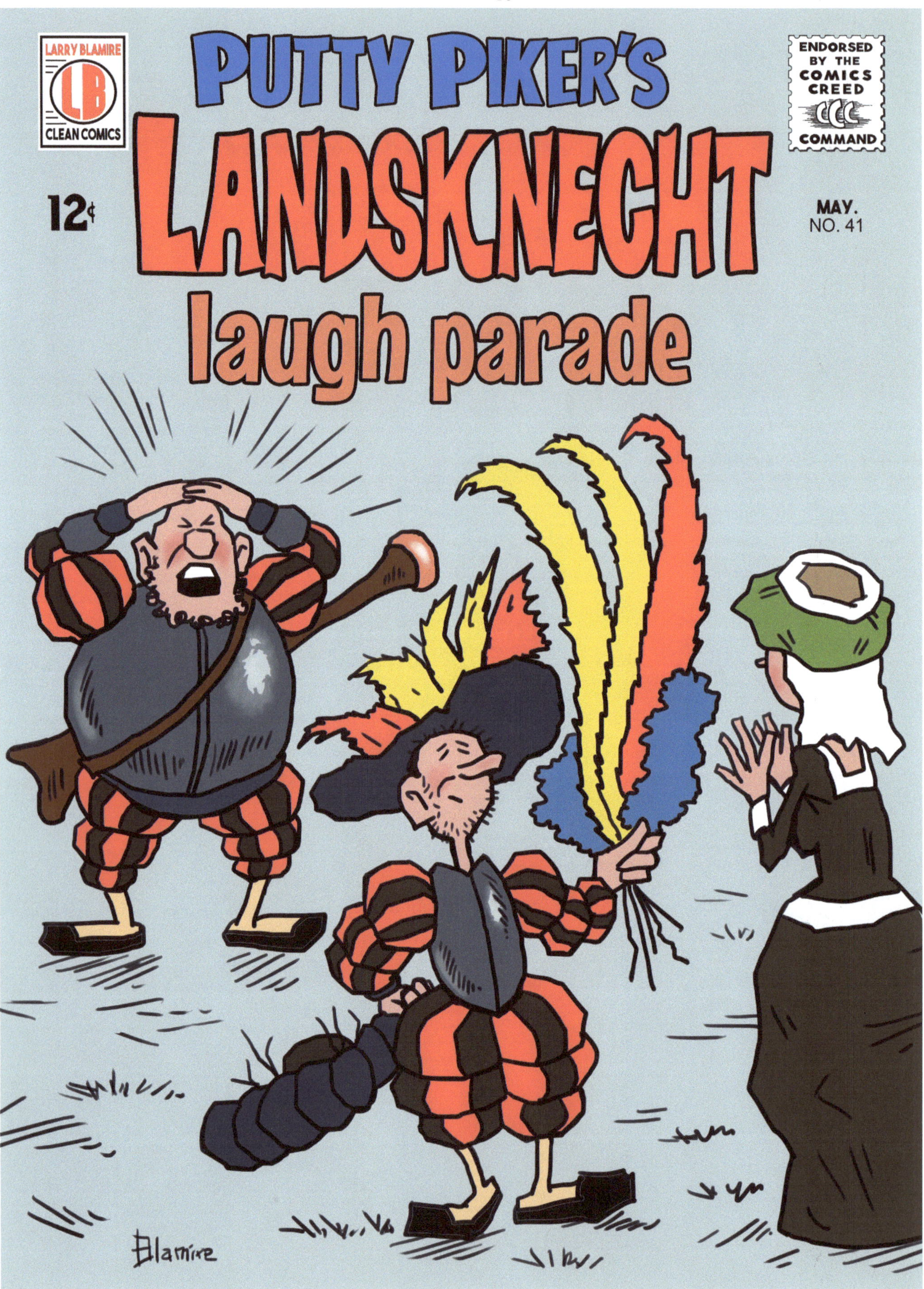
LARRY BLAMIRE
LB
CLEAN COMICS
PUTTY PIKER'S
LANDSKNECHT
laugh parade
ENDORSED BY THE COMICS CREED
CCC
COMMAND
12¢
MAY.
NO. 41
Blamire

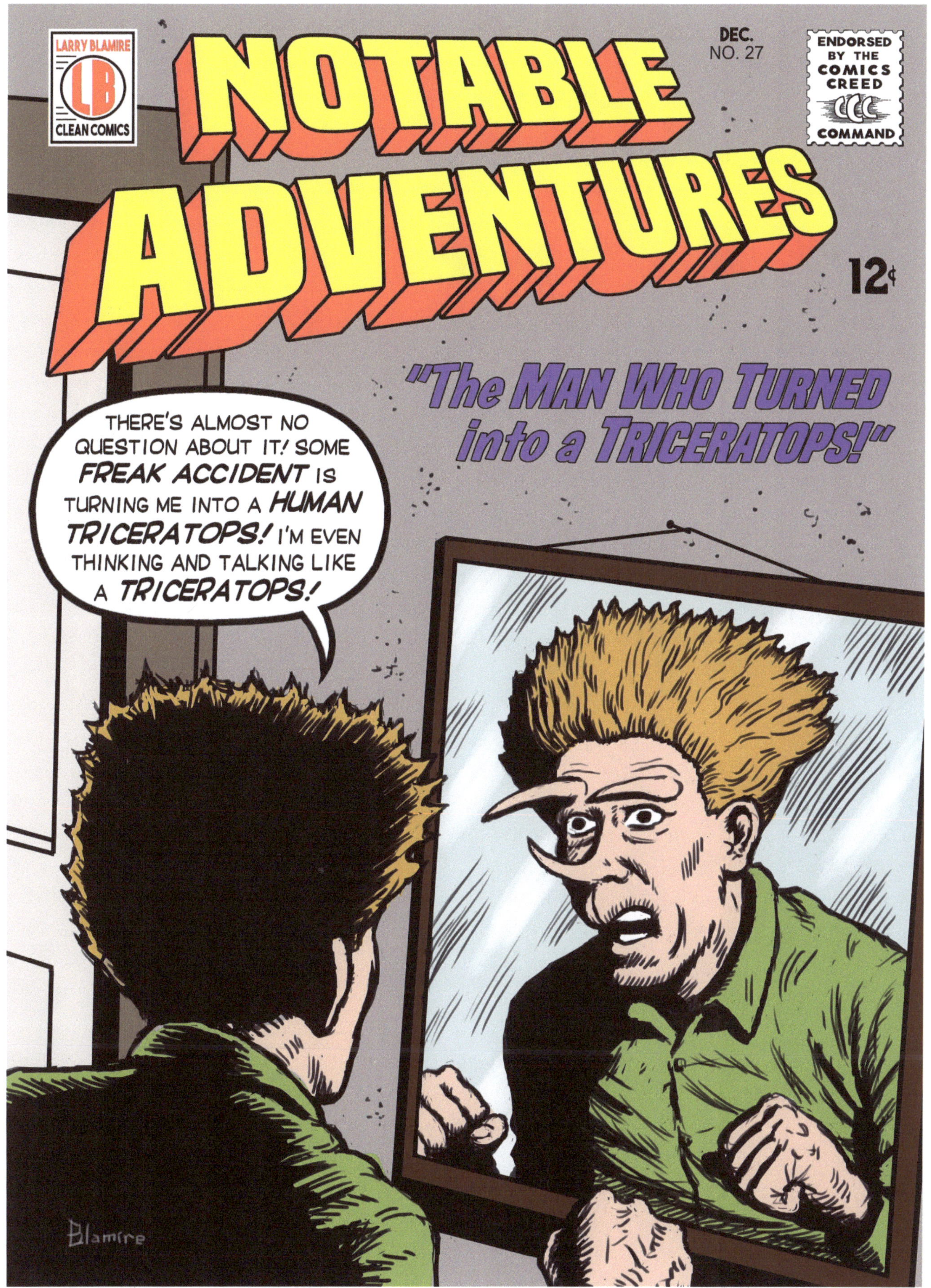
LARRY BLAMIRE
LB
CLEAN COMICS
NOTABLE ADVENTURES
DEC.
NO. 27
ENDORSED BY THE COMICS CREED
CCC
COMMAND
12¢
"The MAN WHO TURNED into a TRICERATOPS!"
THERE'S ALMOST NO QUESTION ABOUT IT! SOME FREAK ACCIDENT IS TURNING ME INTO A HUMAN TRICERATOPS! I'M EVEN THINKING AND TALKING LIKE A TRICERATOPS!
Blamire

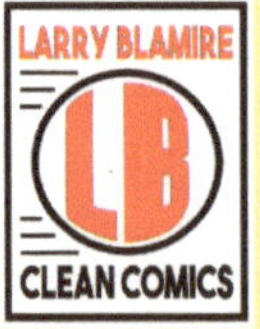

FEB.
NO. 71

ENDORSED BY THE COMICS CREED COMMAND

12¢

Little Reaper

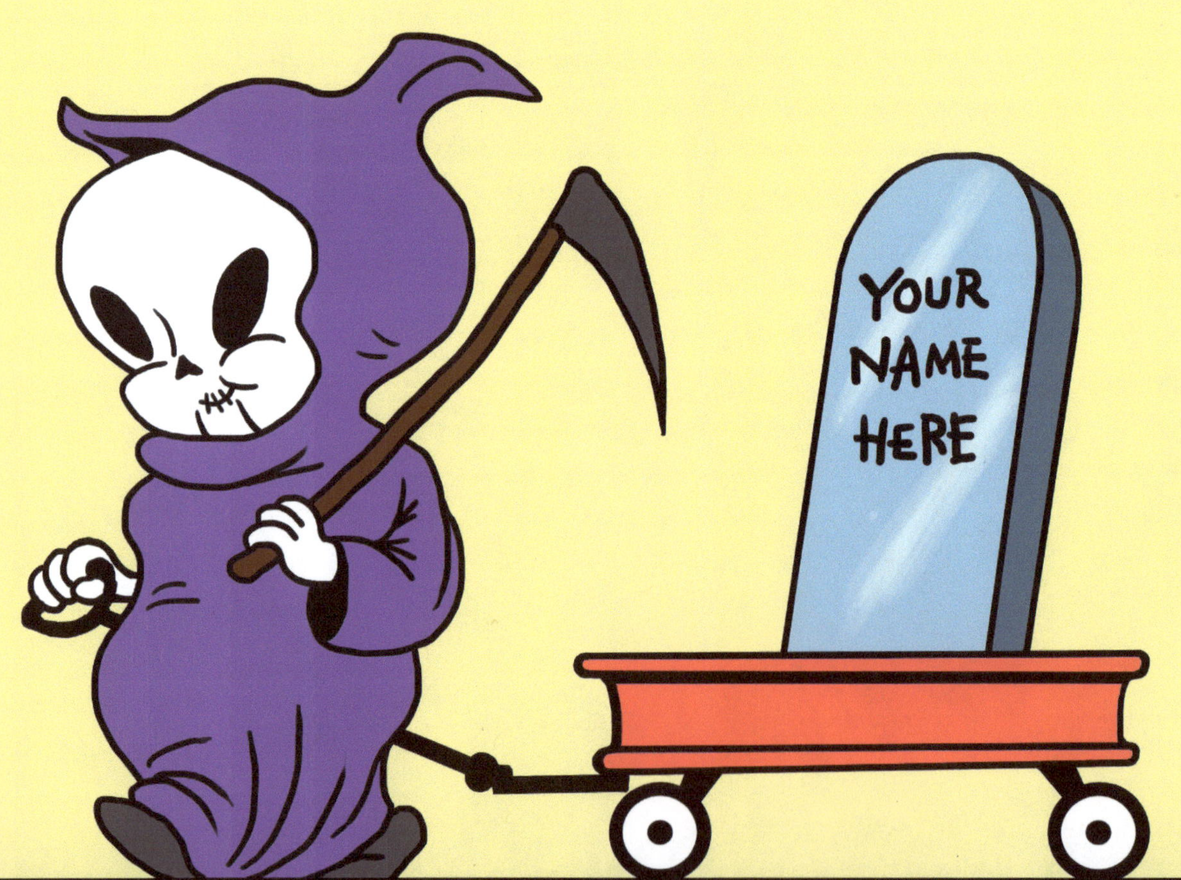

Blamire

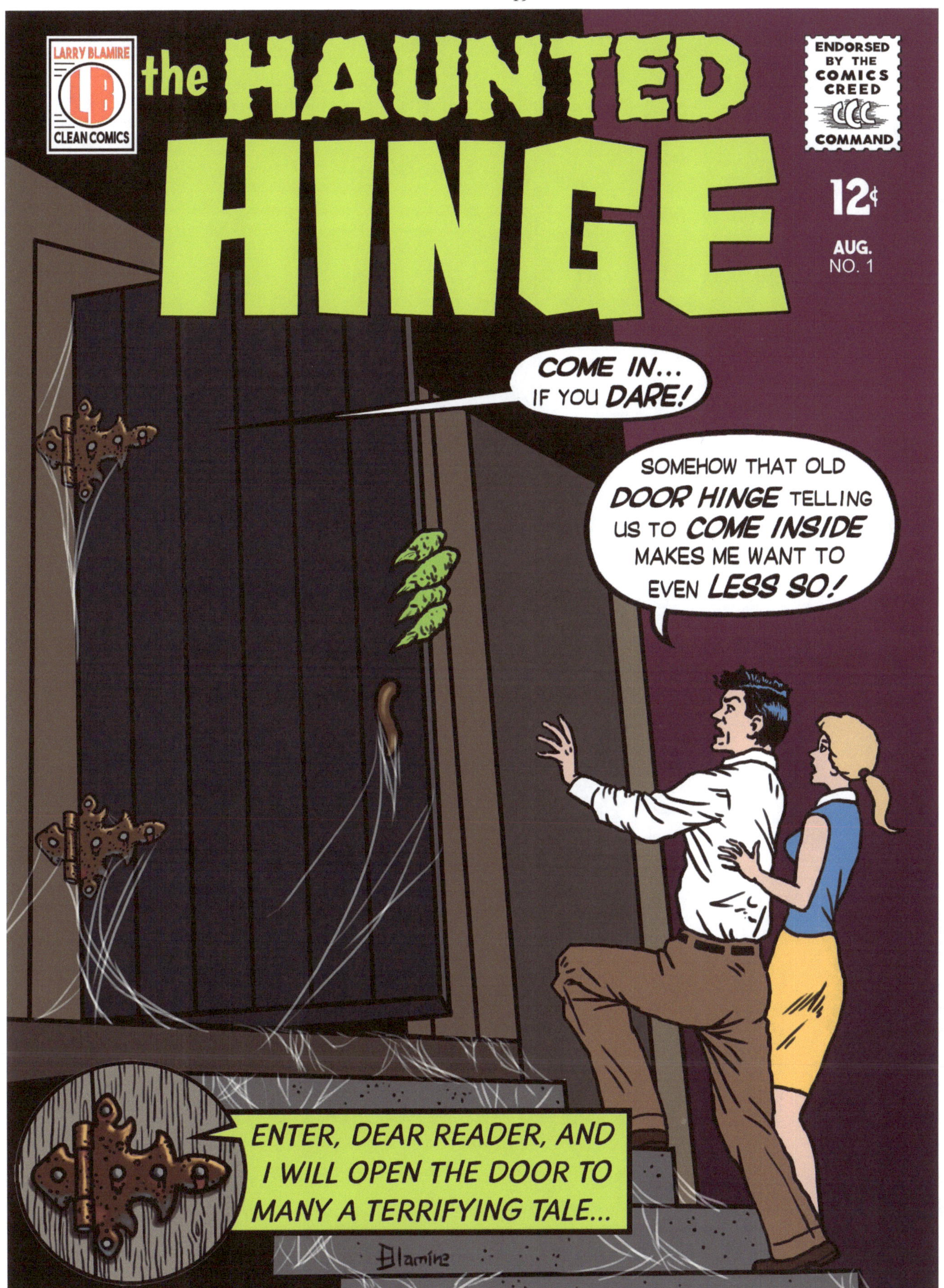
LARRY BLAMIRE
LB
CLEAN COMICS
the HAUNTED HINGE
ENDORSED BY THE COMICS CREED CCC COMMAND
12¢
AUG.
NO. 1
COME IN... IF YOU DARE!
SOMEHOW THAT OLD DOOR HINGE TELLING US TO COME INSIDE MAKES ME WANT TO EVEN LESS SO!
ENTER, DEAR READER, AND I WILL OPEN THE DOOR TO MANY A TERRIFYING TALE...
Blamire

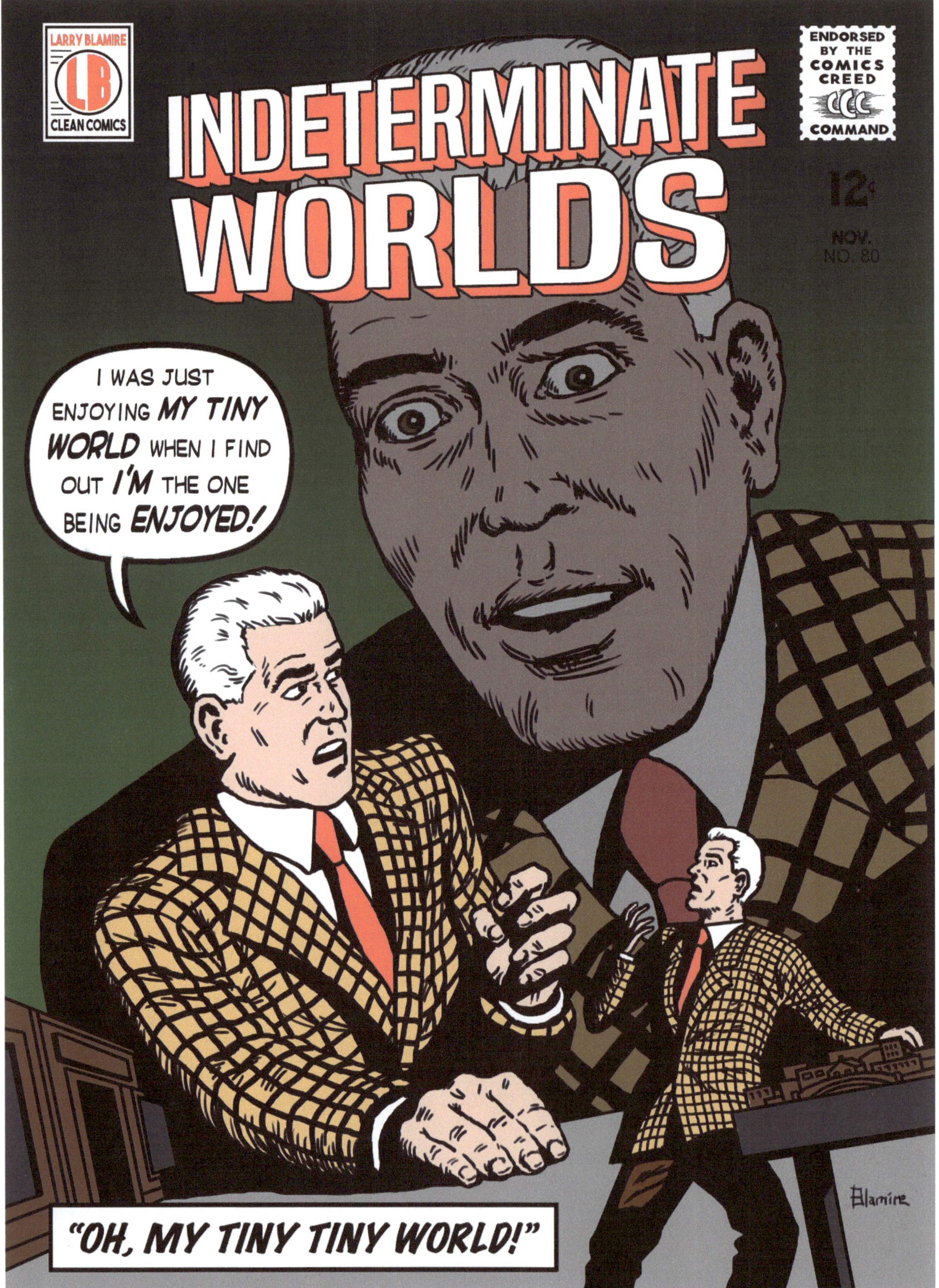
LARRY BLAMIRE
LB
CLEAN COMICS
INDETERMINATE WORLDS
ENDORSED BY THE COMICS CREED CCC COMMAND
12¢
NOV.
NO. 80
I WAS JUST ENJOYING MY TINY WORLD WHEN I FIND OUT I'M THE ONE BEING ENJOYED!
Blamire
"OH, MY TINY TINY WORLD!"

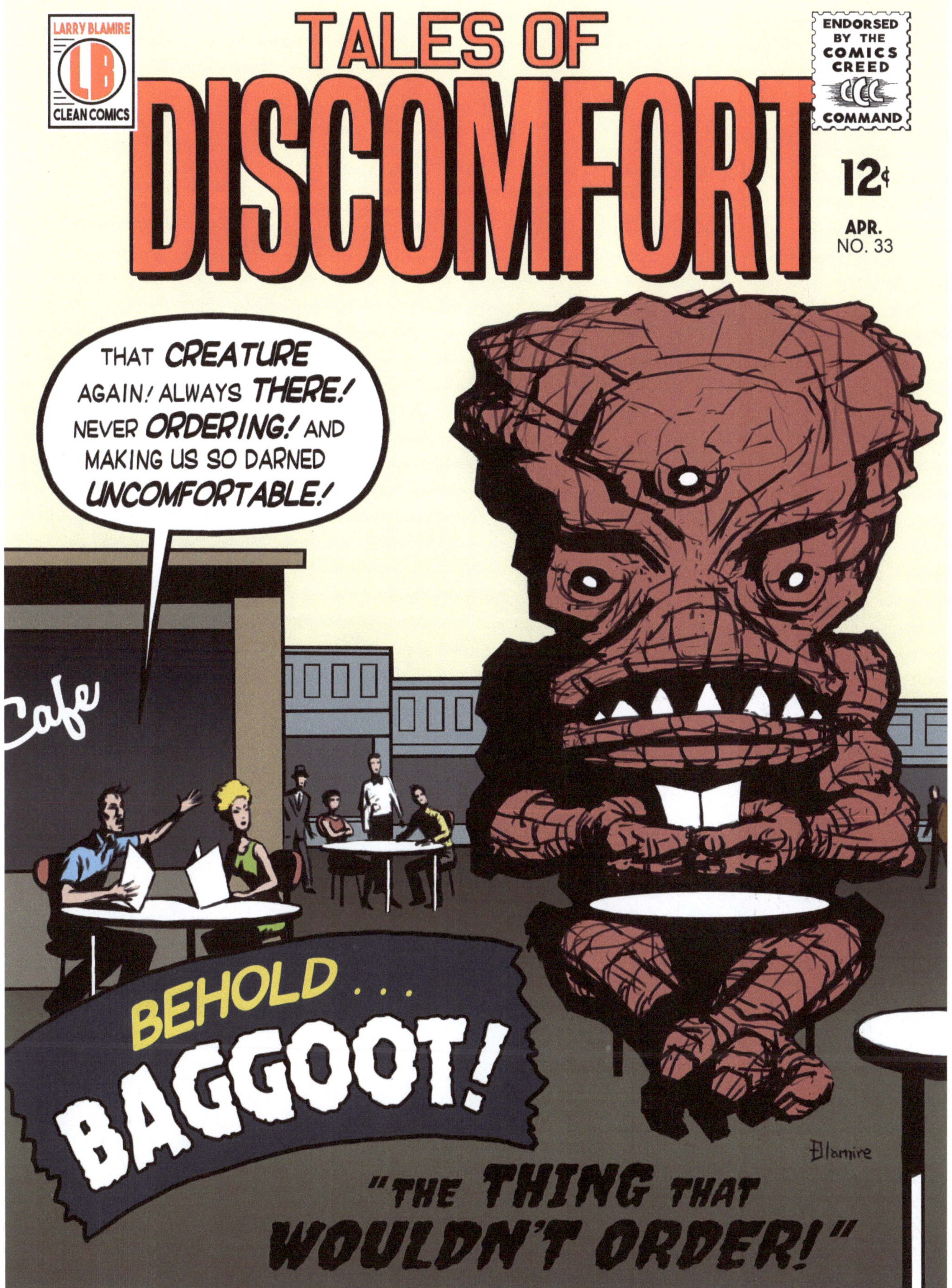
LARRY BLAMIRE
LB
CLEAN COMICS
TALES OF
DISCOMFORT
ENDORSED BY THE COMICS CREED
CCC
COMMAND
12¢
APR.
NO. 33
THAT CREATURE AGAIN! ALWAYS THERE! NEVER ORDERING! AND MAKING US SO DARNED UNCOMFORTABLE!
Cafe
BEHOLD . . .
BAGGOOT!
Blamire
"THE THING THAT WOULDN'T ORDER!"

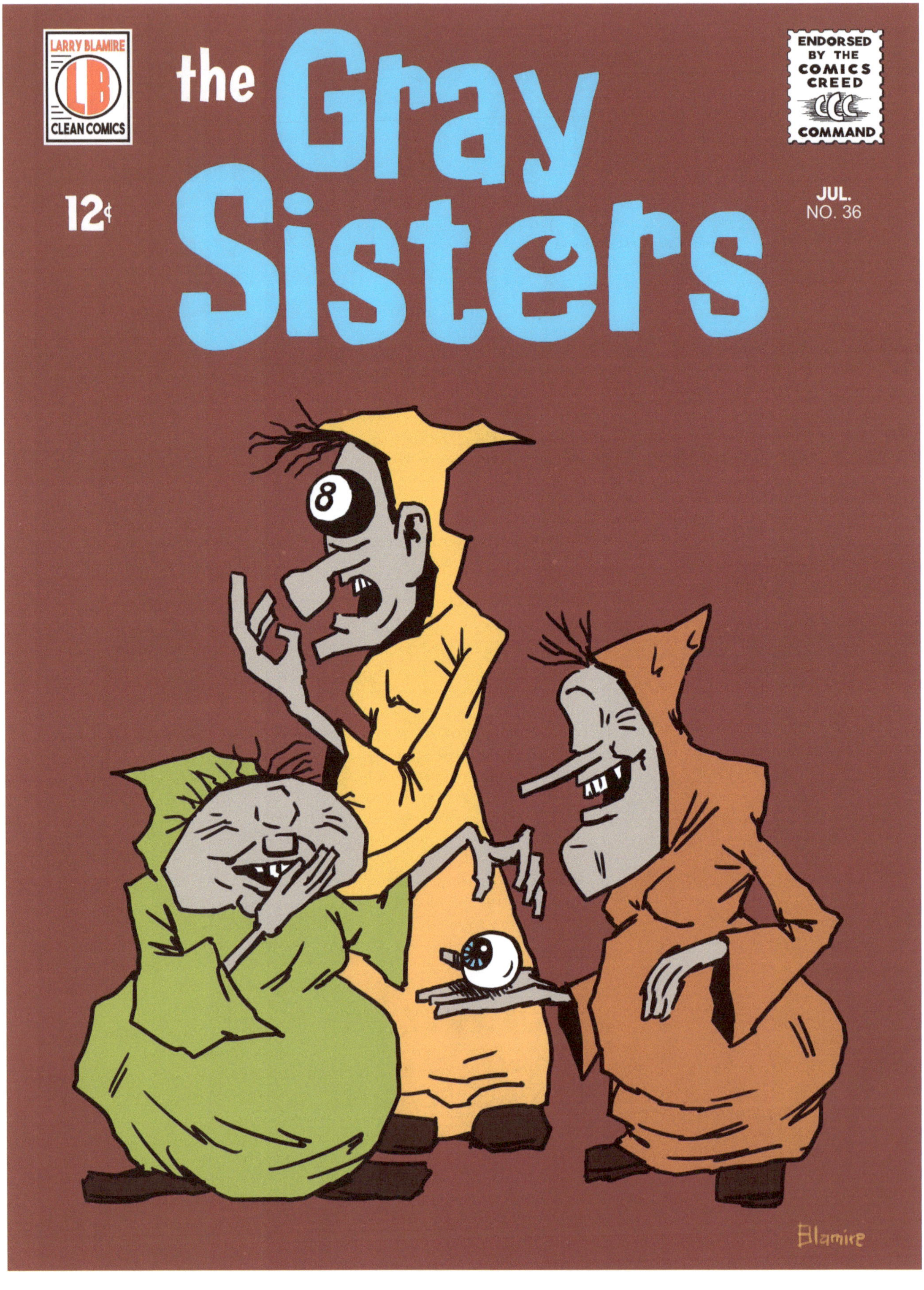

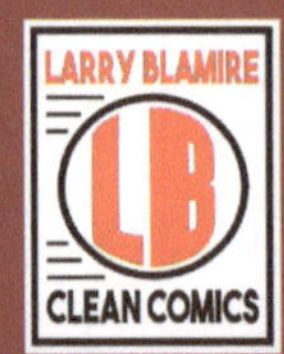

ENDORSED BY THE COMICS CREED COMMAND

the Gray Sisters

12¢

JUL.
NO. 36

Blamire

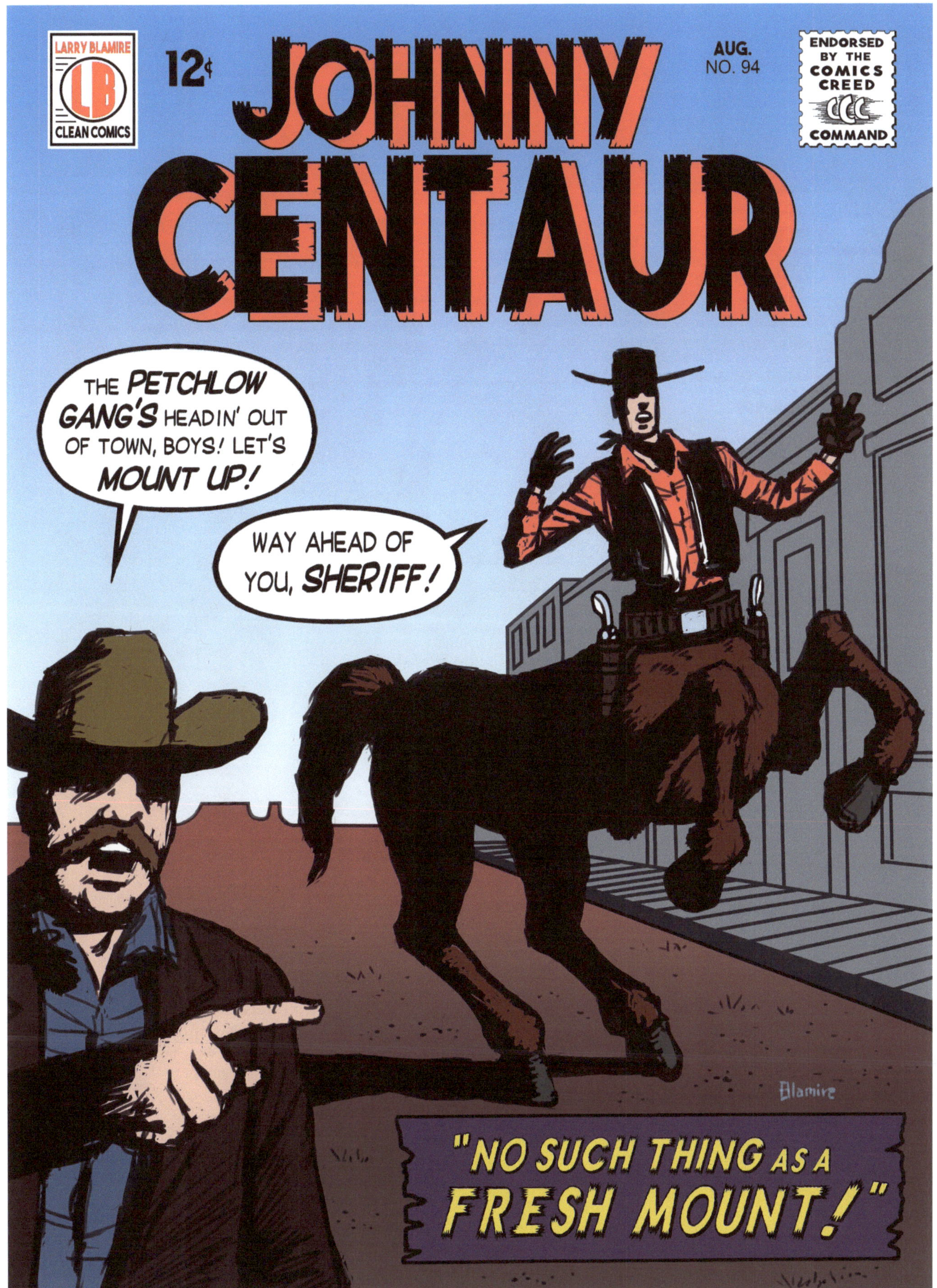
LARRY BLAMIRE
LB
CLEAN COMICS
12¢
JOHNNY CENTAUR
AUG.
NO. 94
ENDORSED BY THE COMICS CREED
CCC
COMMAND
THE PETCHLOW GANG'S HEADIN' OUT OF TOWN, BOYS! LET'S MOUNT UP!
WAY AHEAD OF YOU, SHERIFF!
Blamire
"NO SUCH THING AS A FRESH MOUNT!"

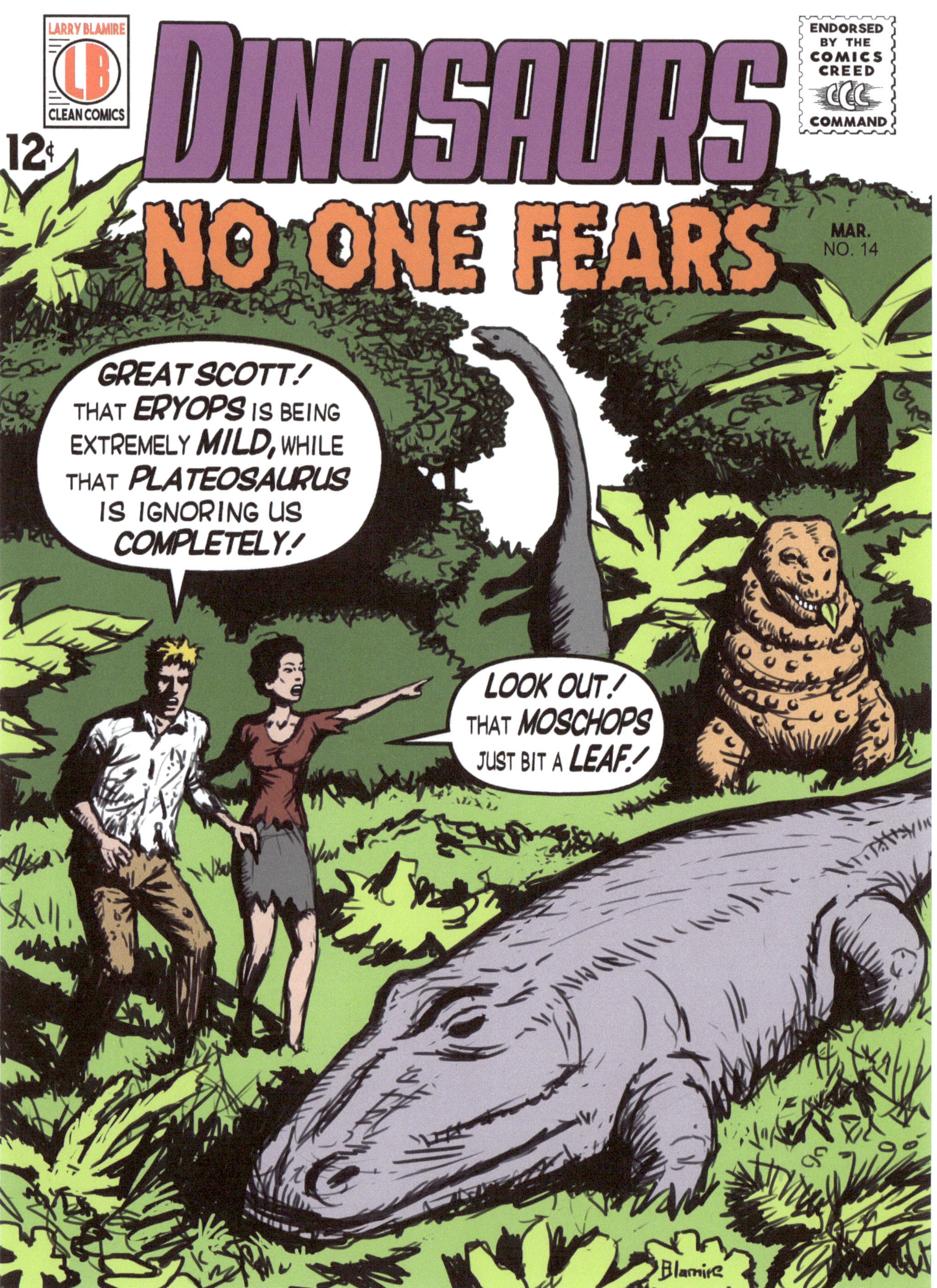
LARRY BLAMIRE
LB
CLEAN COMICS
12¢
DINOSAURS
NO ONE FEARS
ENDORSED BY THE COMICS CREED
CCC
COMMAND
MAR.
NO. 14
GREAT SCOTT! THAT ERYOPS IS BEING EXTREMELY MILD, WHILE THAT PLATEOSAURUS IS IGNORING US COMPLETELY!
LOOK OUT! THAT MOSCHOPS JUST BIT A LEAF!
Blamire

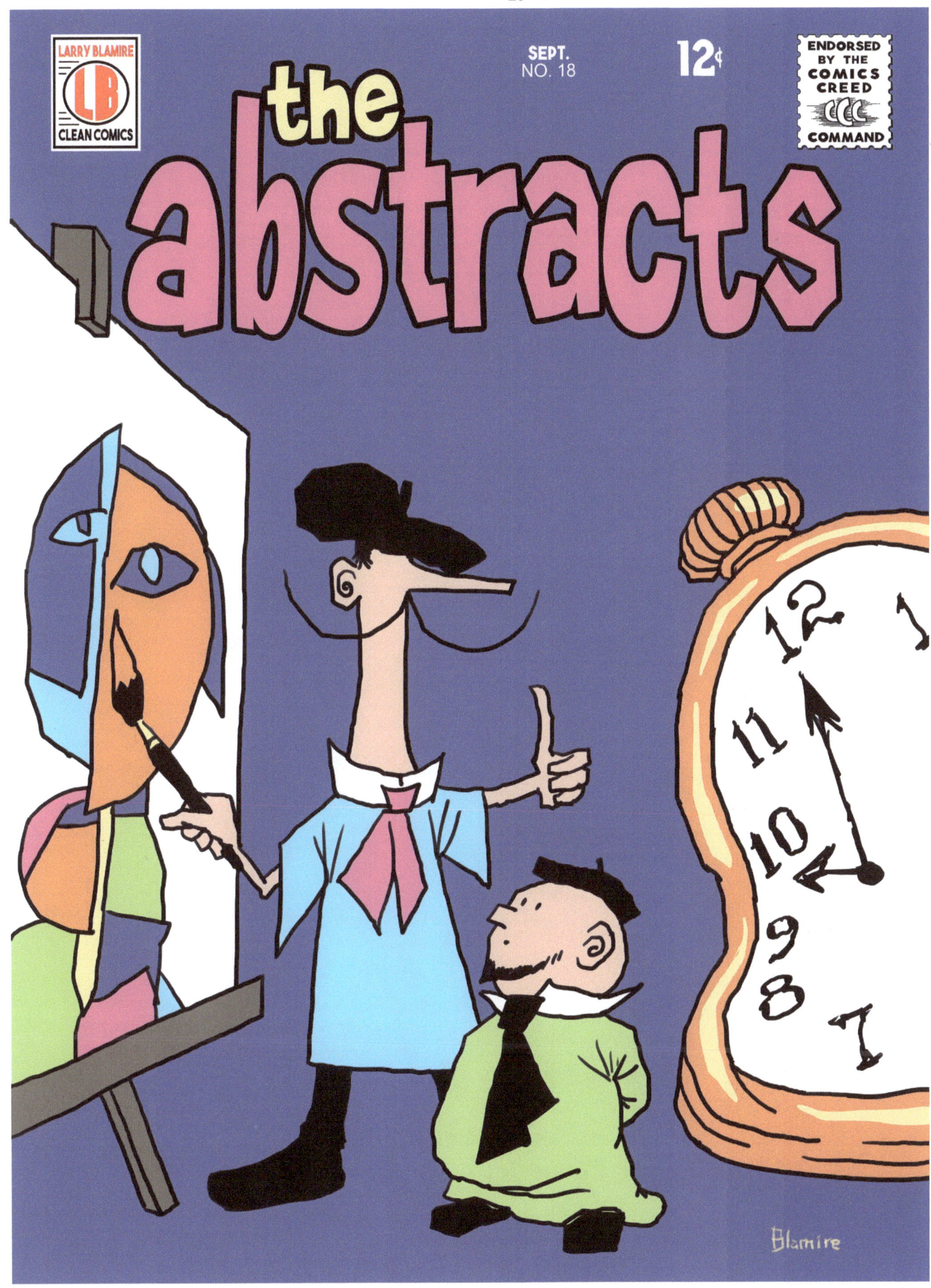
LARRY BLAMIRE
LB
CLEAN COMICS
SEPT.
NO. 18
12¢
ENDORSED BY THE COMICS CREED
CCC
COMMAND
the abstracts
Blamire

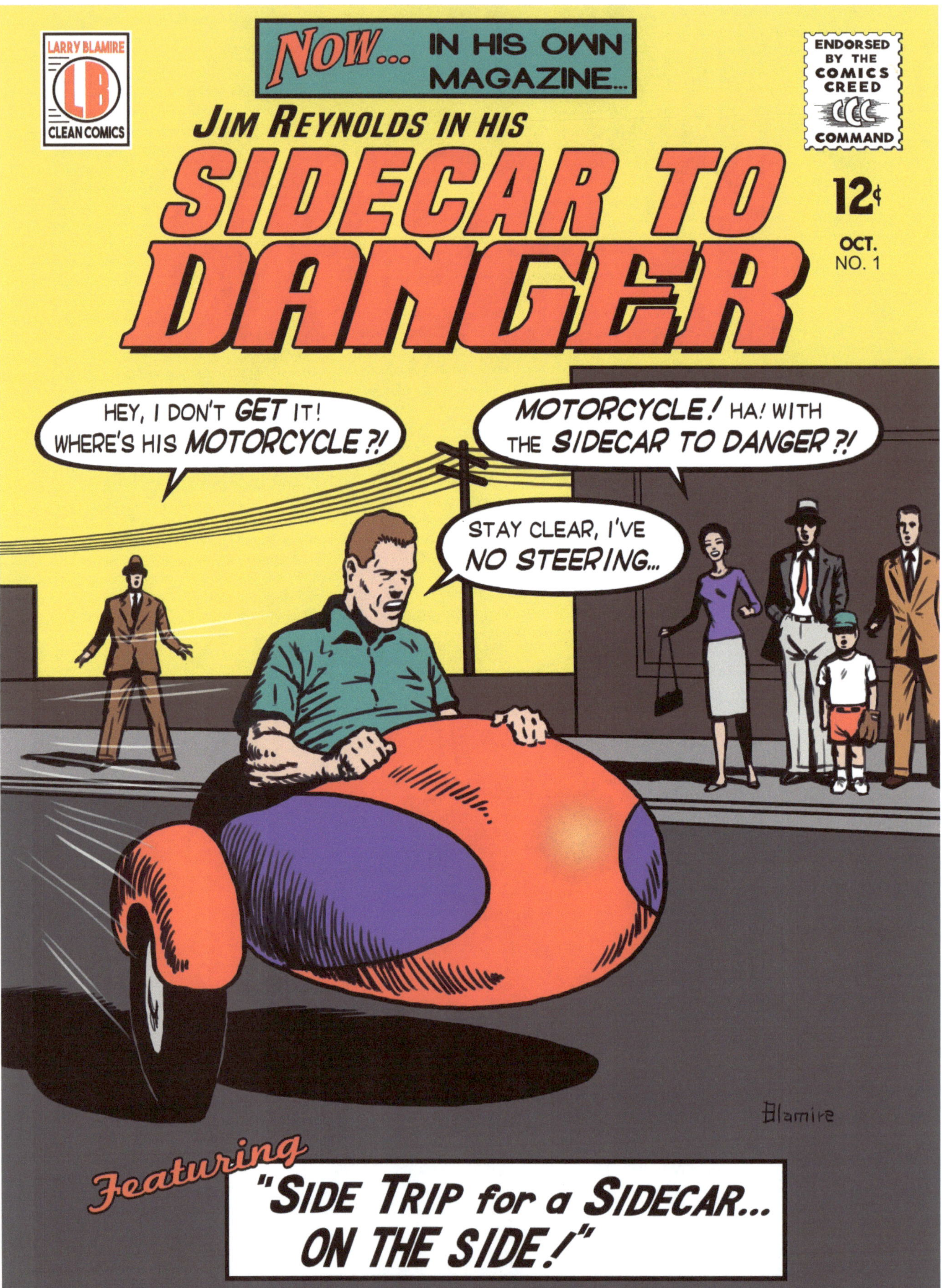
LARRY BLAMIRE
LB
CLEAN COMICS
NOW... IN HIS OWN MAGAZINE...
ENDORSED BY THE COMICS CREED
CCC
COMMAND
JIM REYNOLDS IN HIS
SIDECAR TO DANGER
12¢
OCT.
NO. 1
HEY, I DON'T GET IT! WHERE'S HIS MOTORCYCLE?!
MOTORCYCLE! HA! WITH THE SIDECAR TO DANGER?!
STAY CLEAR, I'VE NO STEERING...
Blamire
Featuring
"SIDE TRIP for a SIDECAR... ON THE SIDE!"

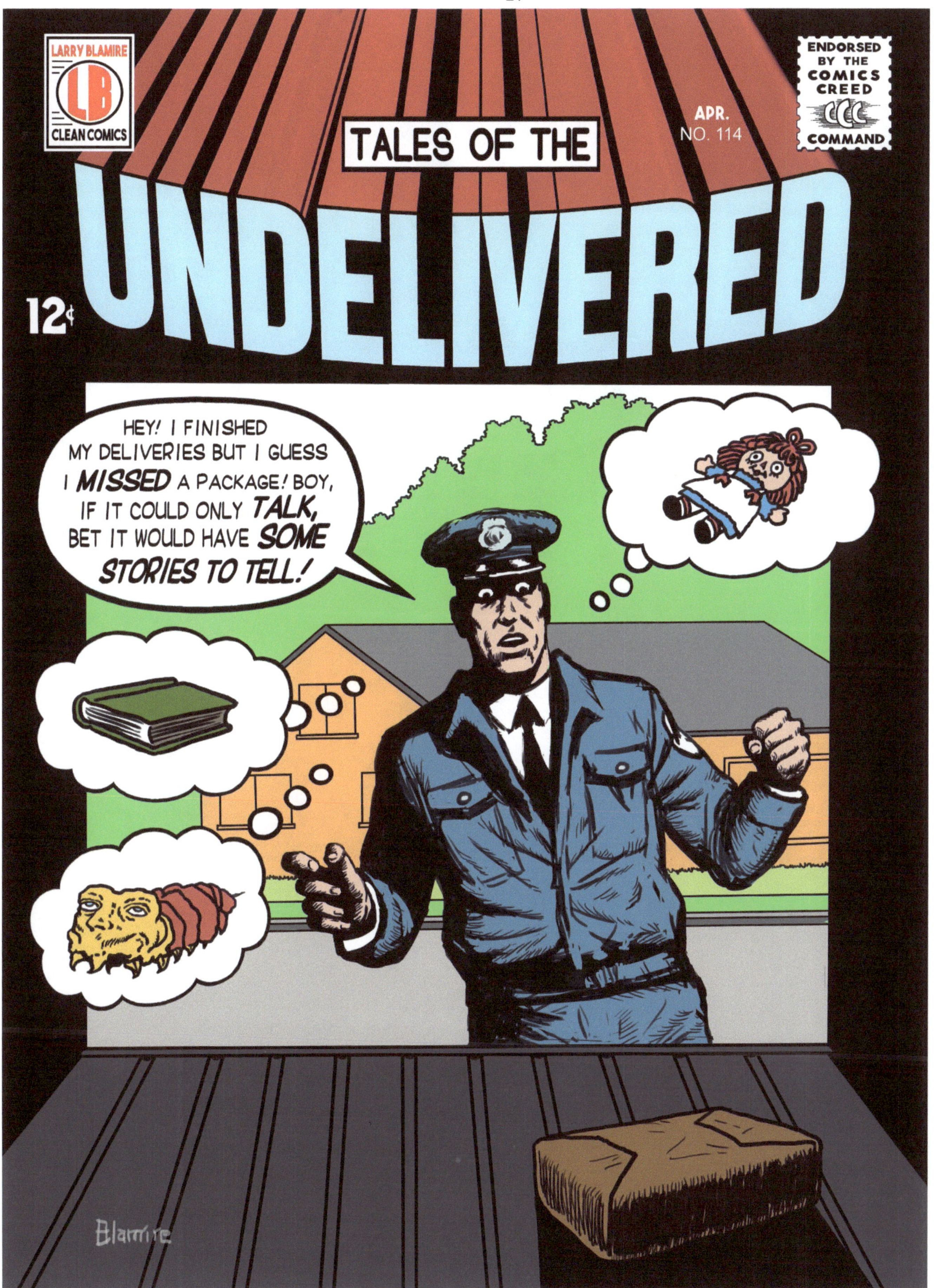
LARRY BLAMIRE
LB
CLEAN COMICS
TALES OF THE
UNDELIVERED
APR.
NO. 114
ENDORSED BY THE COMICS CREED
CCC
COMMAND
12¢
HEY! I FINISHED MY DELIVERIES BUT I GUESS I MISSED A PACKAGE! BOY, IF IT COULD ONLY TALK, BET IT WOULD HAVE SOME STORIES TO TELL!
Blamire

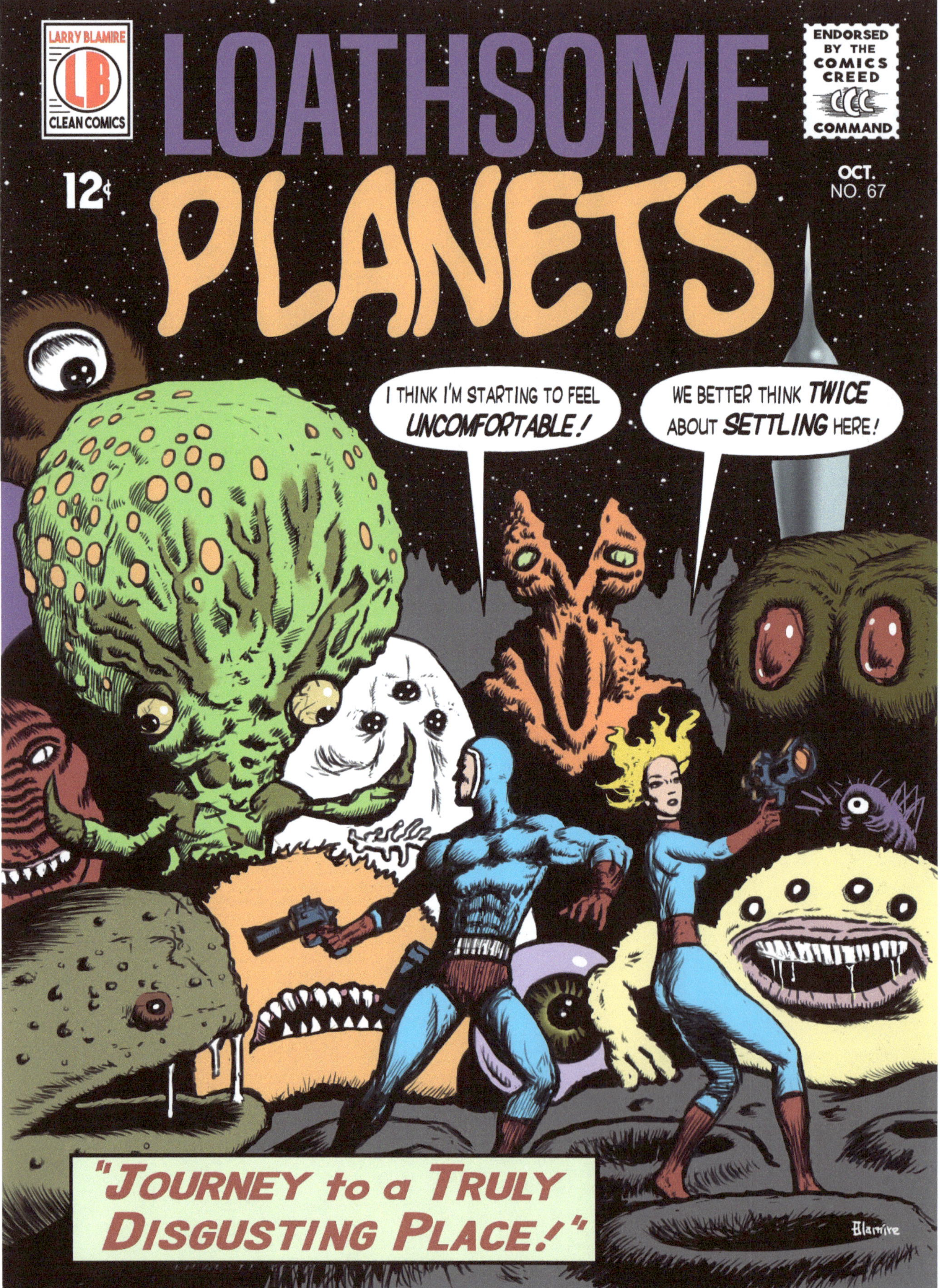
LARRY BLAMIRE
LB
CLEAN COMICS
LOATHSOME
PLANETS
ENDORSED BY THE COMICS CREED
CCC
COMMAND
12¢
OCT.
NO. 67
I THINK I'M STARTING TO FEEL UNCOMFORTABLE!
WE BETTER THINK TWICE ABOUT SETTLING HERE!
"JOURNEY to a TRULY DISGUSTING PLACE!"
Blamire

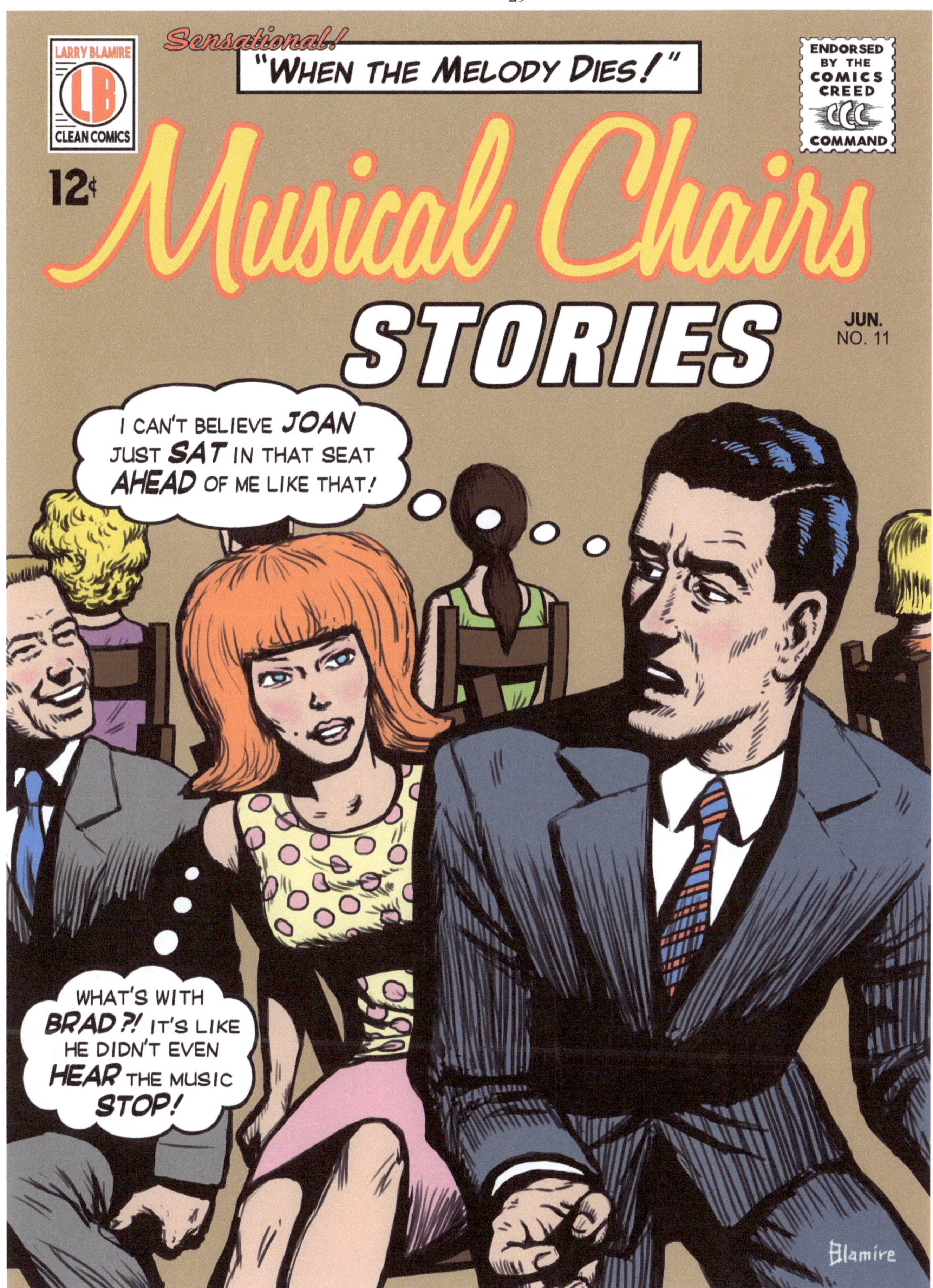
LARRY BLAMIRE
LB
CLEAN COMICS
12¢
Sensational!
"WHEN THE MELODY DIES!"
ENDORSED BY THE COMICS CREED
CCC
COMMAND
Musical Chairs
STORIES
JUN.
NO. 11
I CAN'T BELIEVE JOAN JUST SAT IN THAT SEAT AHEAD OF ME LIKE THAT!
WHAT'S WITH BRAD?! IT'S LIKE HE DIDN'T EVEN HEAR THE MUSIC STOP!
Blamire

LARRY BLAMIRE
LB
CLEAN COMICS
AS SEEN ON TV!
ENDORSED BY THE COMICS CREED
CCC
COMMAND
THE PINE NUTS
12¢
AUG.
NO. 4
with SPRUCE, CONNIE and little DOUGLAS FIR

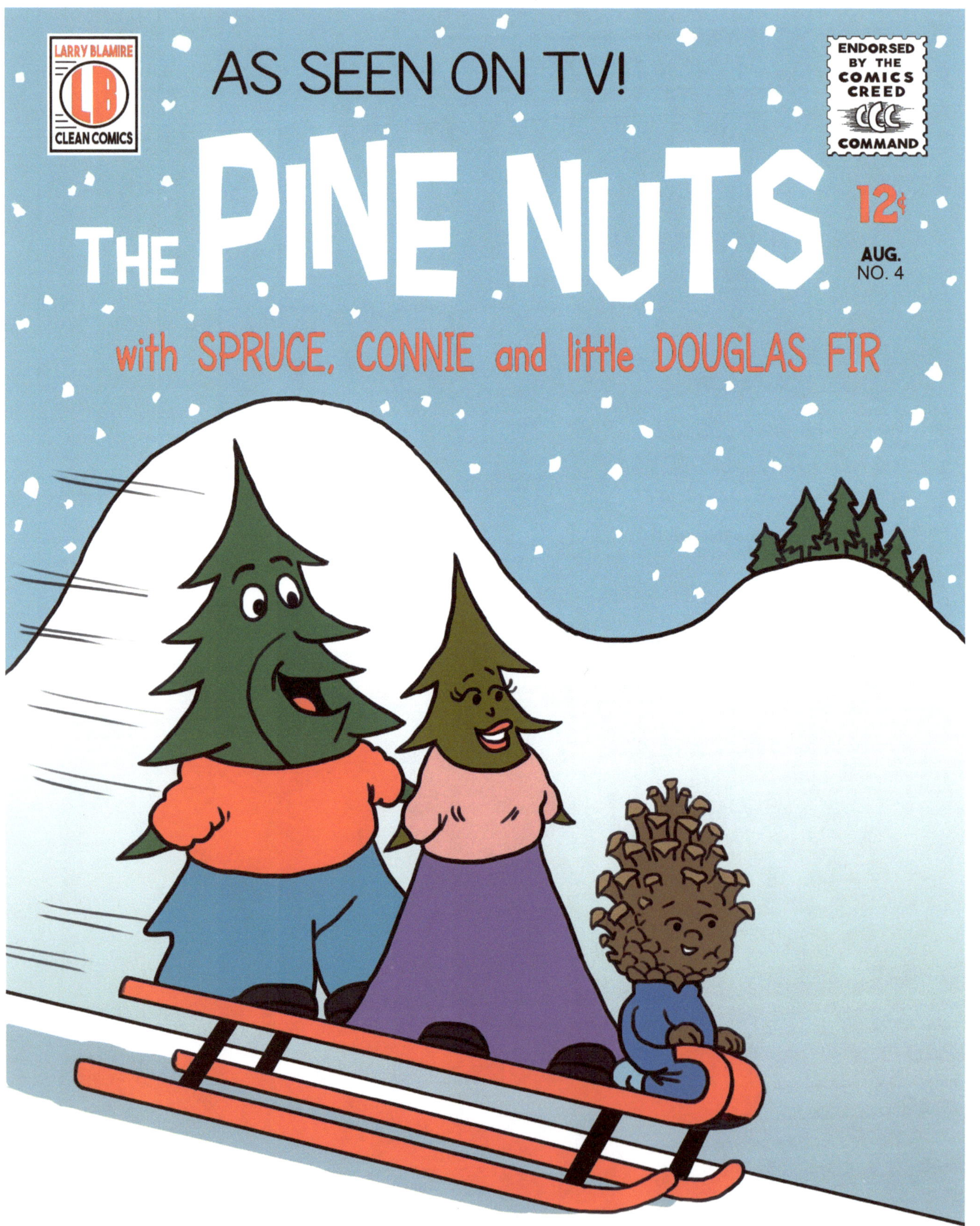

Blamire

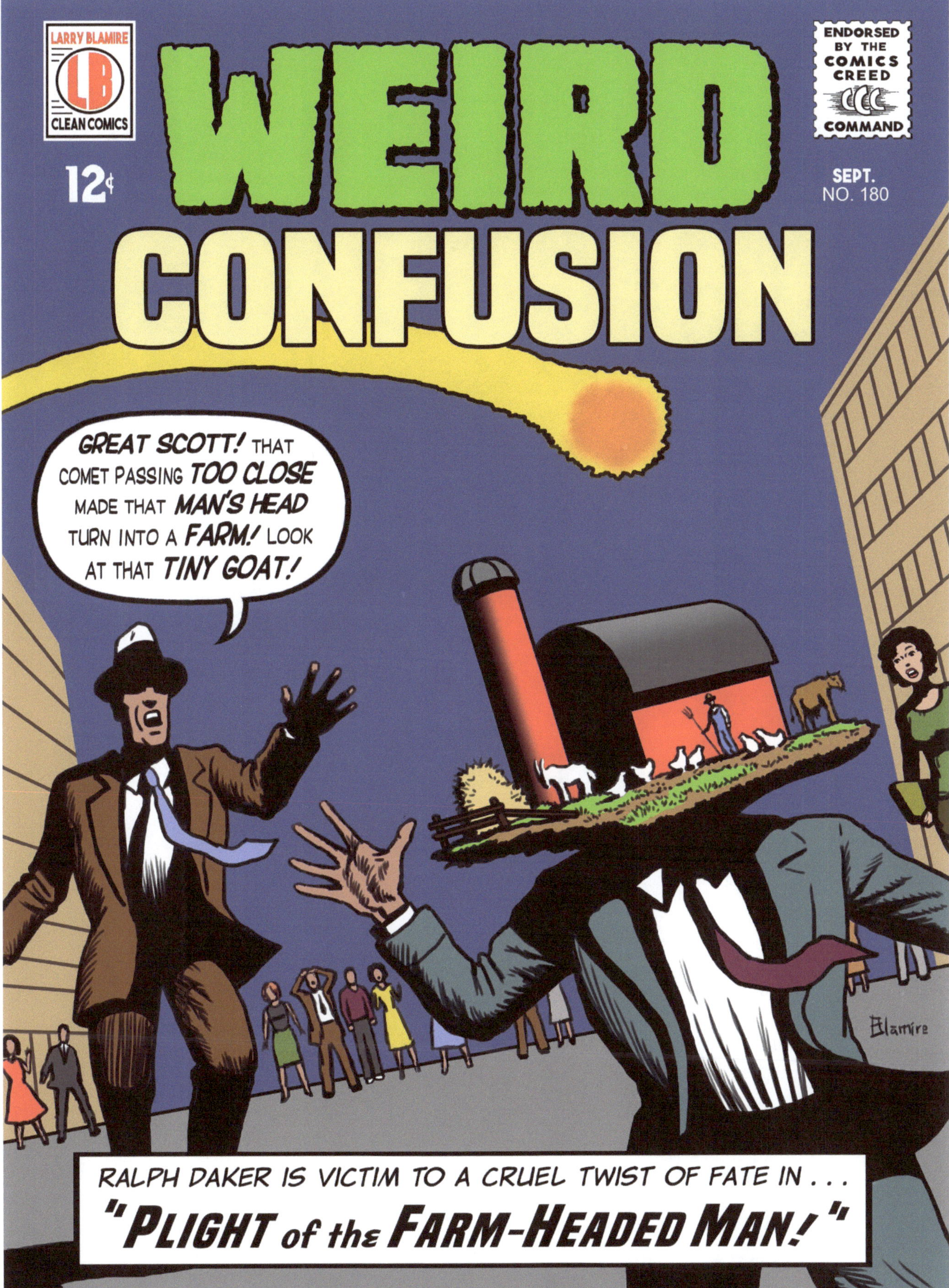
LARRY BLAMIRE
LB
CLEAN COMICS
WEIRD
CONFUSION
ENDORSED BY THE COMICS CREED
CCC
COMMAND
12¢
SEPT.
NO. 180
GREAT SCOTT! THAT COMET PASSING TOO CLOSE MADE THAT MAN'S HEAD TURN INTO A FARM! LOOK AT THAT TINY GOAT!
Blamire
RALPH DAKER IS VICTIM TO A CRUEL TWIST OF FATE IN . . .
"PLIGHT of the FARM-HEADED MAN!"

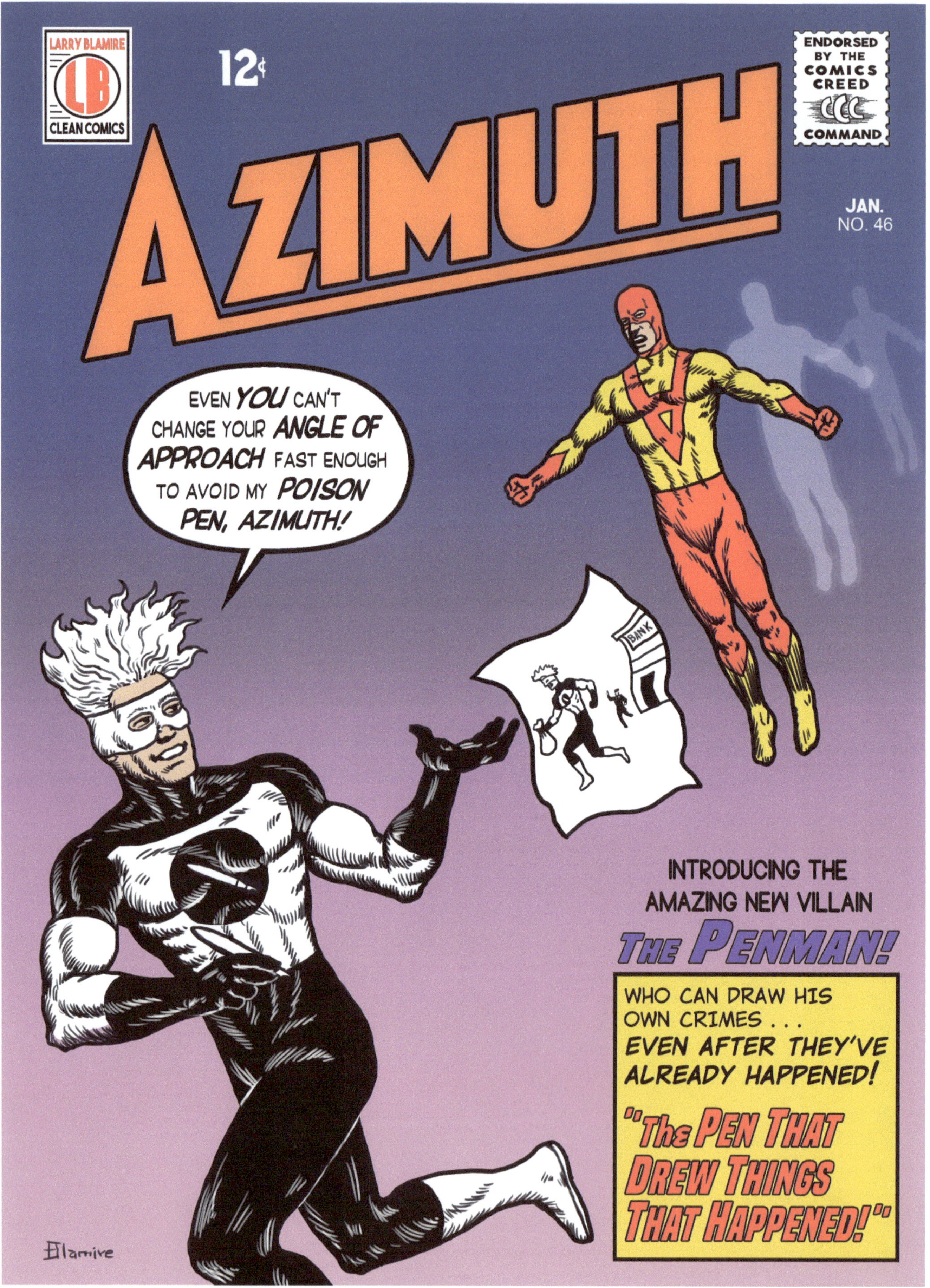
LARRY BLAMIRE
LB
CLEAN COMICS
12¢
ENDORSED BY THE COMICS CREED
CCC
COMMAND
AZIMUTH
JAN.
NO. 46
EVEN YOU CAN'T CHANGE YOUR ANGLE OF APPROACH FAST ENOUGH TO AVOID MY POISON PEN, AZIMUTH!
BANK
INTRODUCING THE AMAZING NEW VILLAIN
THE PENMAN!
WHO CAN DRAW HIS OWN CRIMES . . .
EVEN AFTER THEY'VE ALREADY HAPPENED!
"The PEN THAT DREW THINGS THAT HAPPENED!"
Blamire

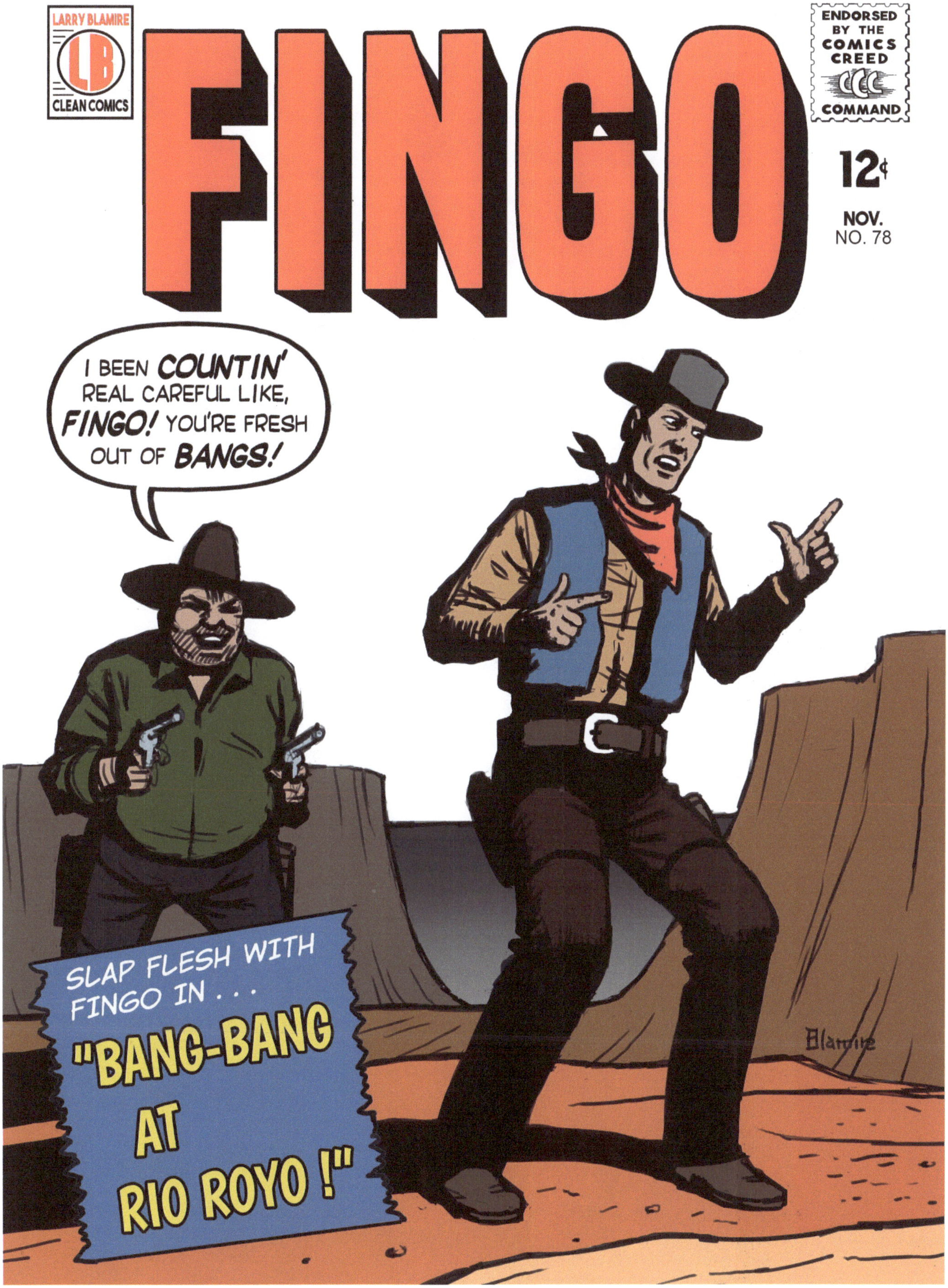

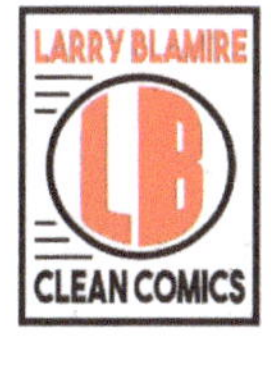

FINGO

ENDORSED BY THE COMICS CREED
CCC
COMMAND

12¢

NOV.
NO. 78

I BEEN **COUNTIN'** REAL CAREFUL LIKE, ***FINGO!*** YOU'RE FRESH OUT OF ***BANGS!***

SLAP FLESH WITH FINGO IN . . .

"BANG-BANG AT RIO ROYO !"

Blamire

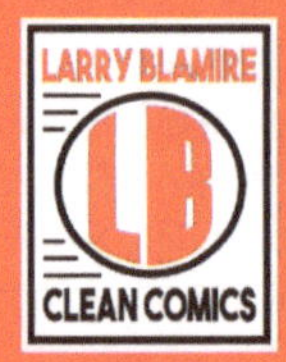

TIME FOR ANOTHER...

12¢

CAP and BULL STORY

ENDORSED BY THE COMICS CREED COMMAND

JAN.
NO. 91

CAP AND BULL MEET MARTIAN PIRATES AFTER SPACE TREASURE!

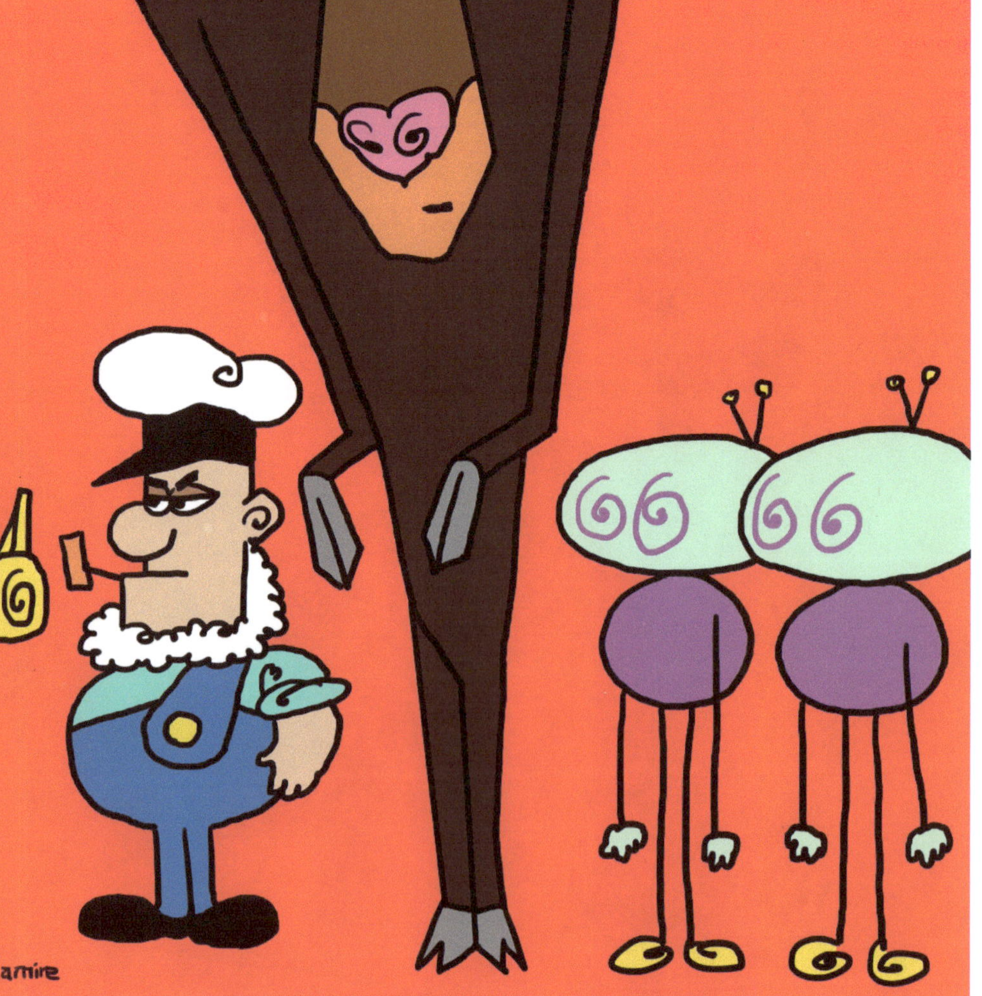

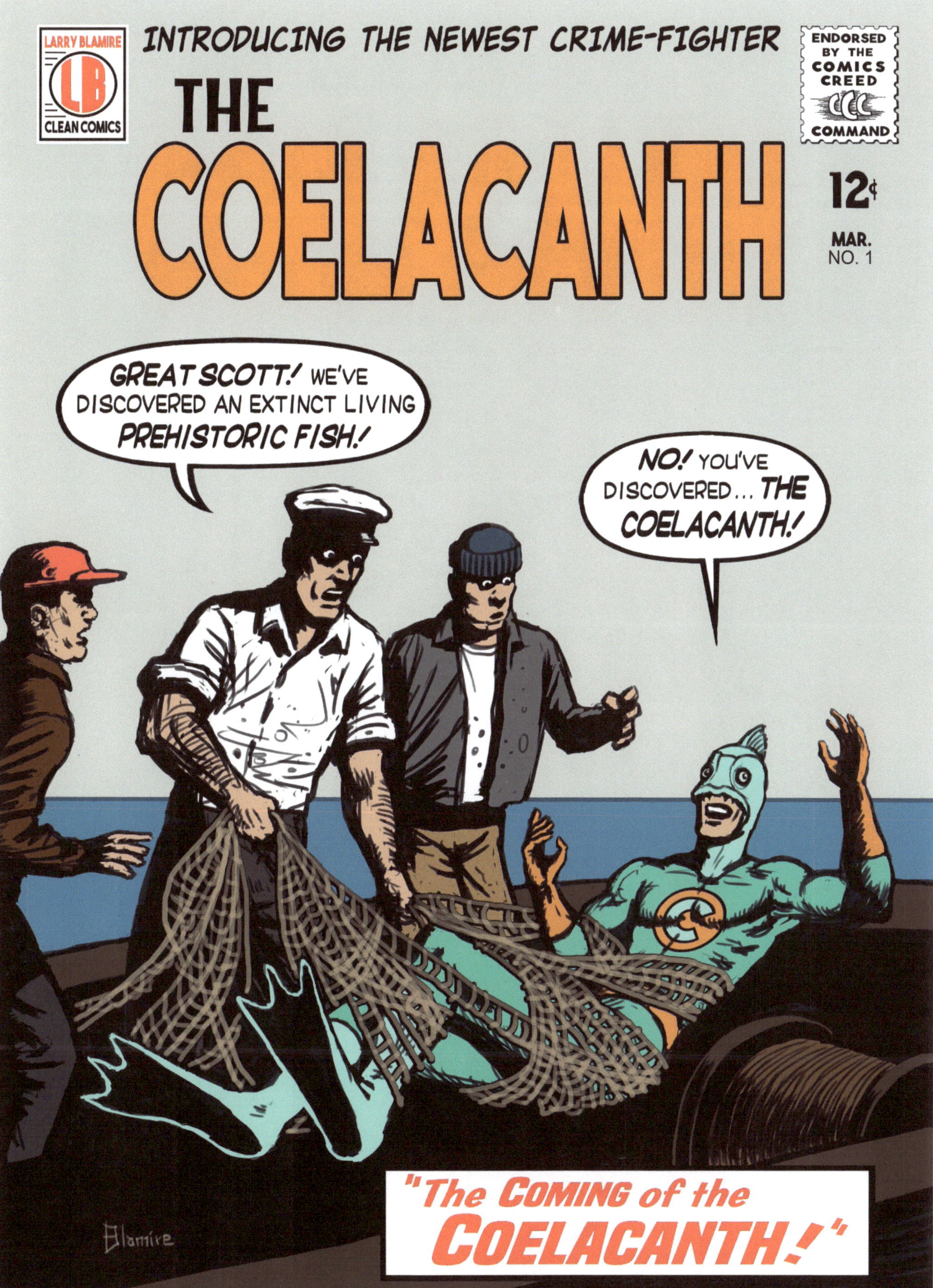
LARRY BLAMIRE
LB
CLEAN COMICS
INTRODUCING THE NEWEST CRIME-FIGHTER
THE COELACANTH
ENDORSED BY THE COMICS CREED
CCC
COMMAND
12¢
MAR.
NO. 1
GREAT SCOTT! WE'VE DISCOVERED AN EXTINCT LIVING PREHISTORIC FISH!
NO! YOU'VE DISCOVERED... THE COELACANTH!
Blamire
"The COMING of the COELACANTH!"

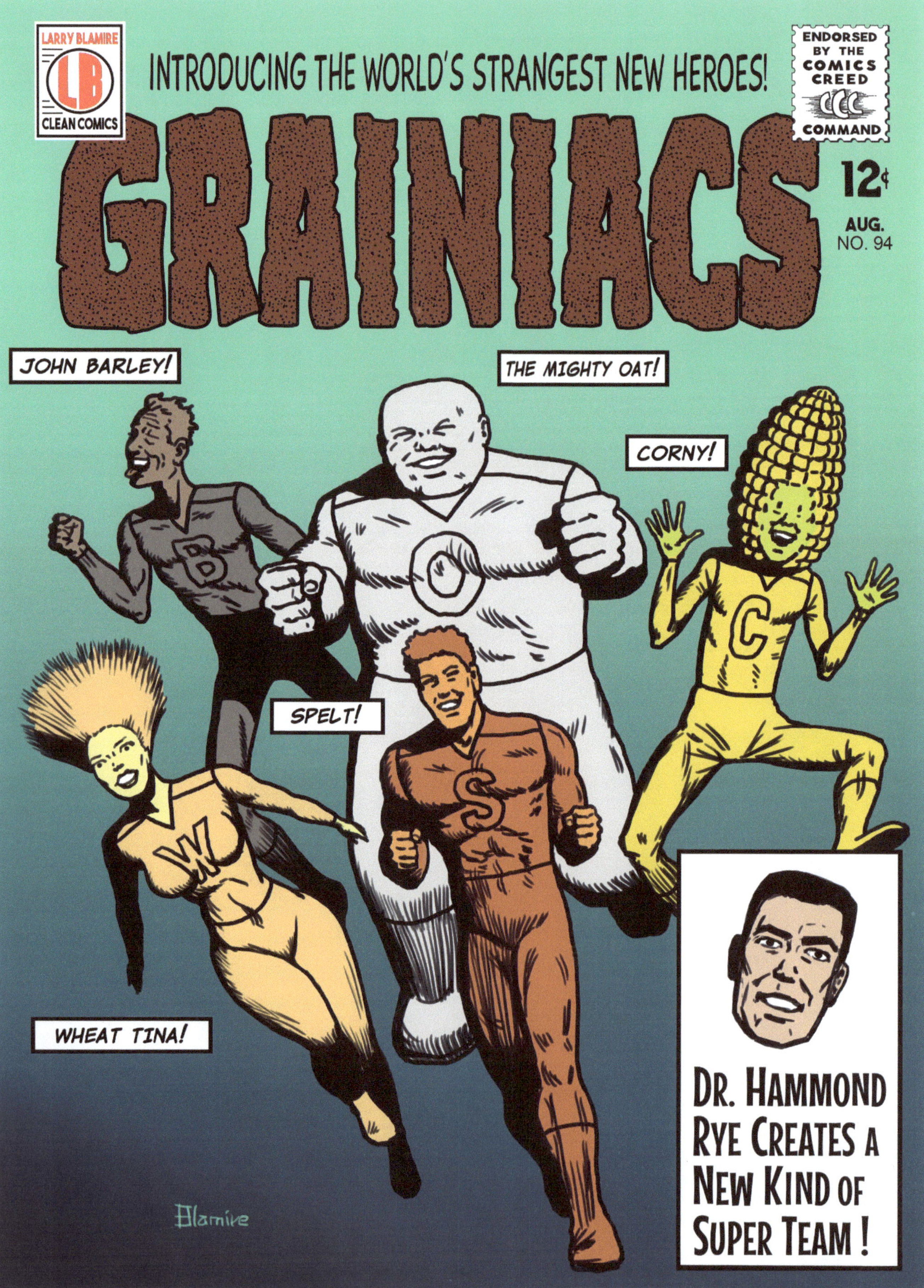
LARRY BLAMIRE
LB
CLEAN COMICS
INTRODUCING THE WORLD'S STRANGEST NEW HEROES!
ENDORSED BY THE COMICS CREED
CCC
COMMAND
GRAINIACS
12¢
AUG.
NO. 94
JOHN BARLEY!
THE MIGHTY OAT!
CORNY!
SPELT!
WHEAT TINA!
DR. HAMMOND RYE CREATES A NEW KIND OF SUPER TEAM!
Blamire

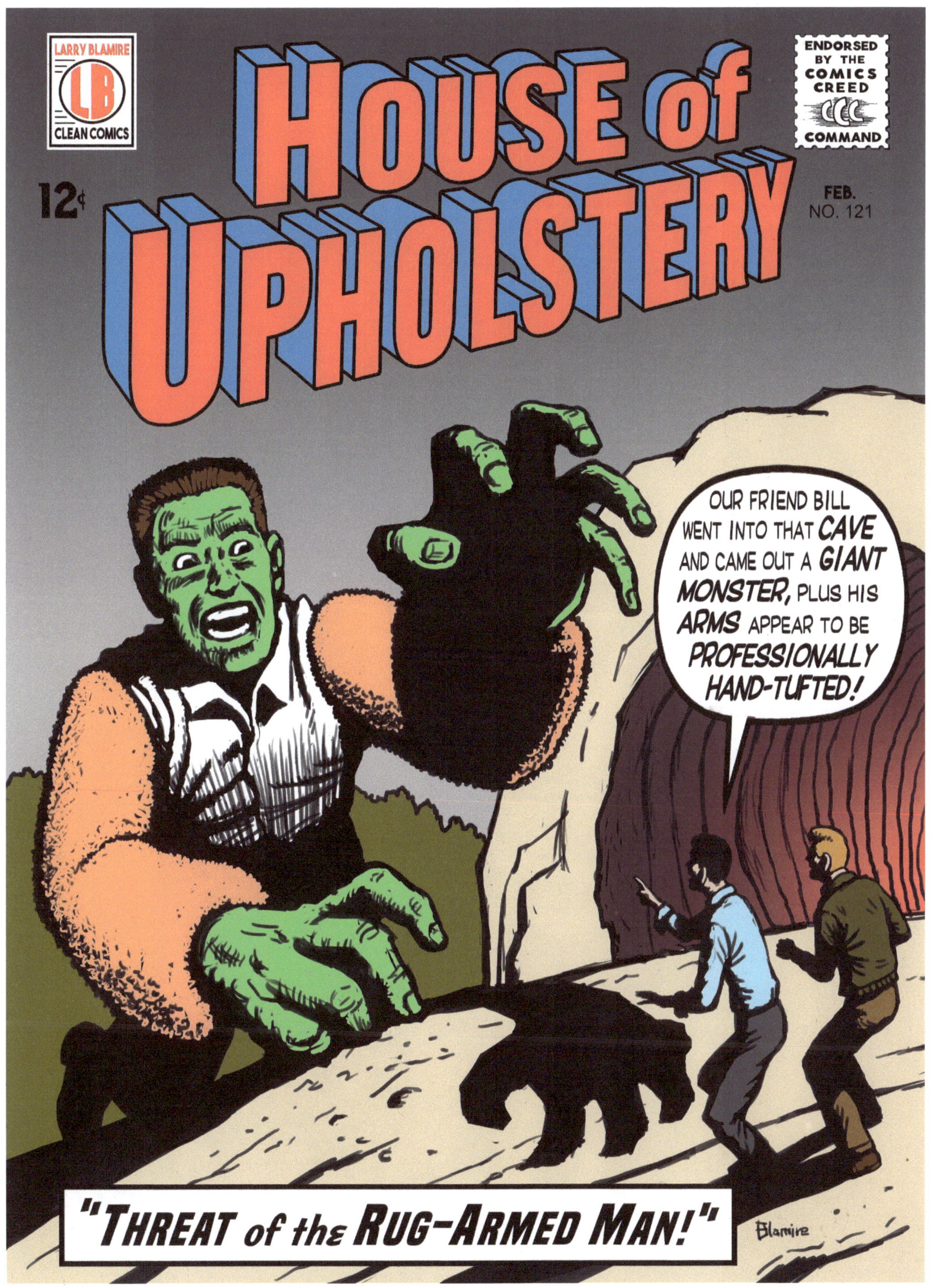
LARRY BLAMIRE
LB
CLEAN COMICS
HOUSE of UPHOLSTERY
ENDORSED BY THE COMICS CREED CCC COMMAND
12¢
FEB.
NO. 121
OUR FRIEND BILL WENT INTO THAT CAVE AND CAME OUT A GIANT MONSTER, PLUS HIS ARMS APPEAR TO BE PROFESSIONALLY HAND-TUFTED!
"THREAT of the RUG-ARMED MAN!"
Blamire

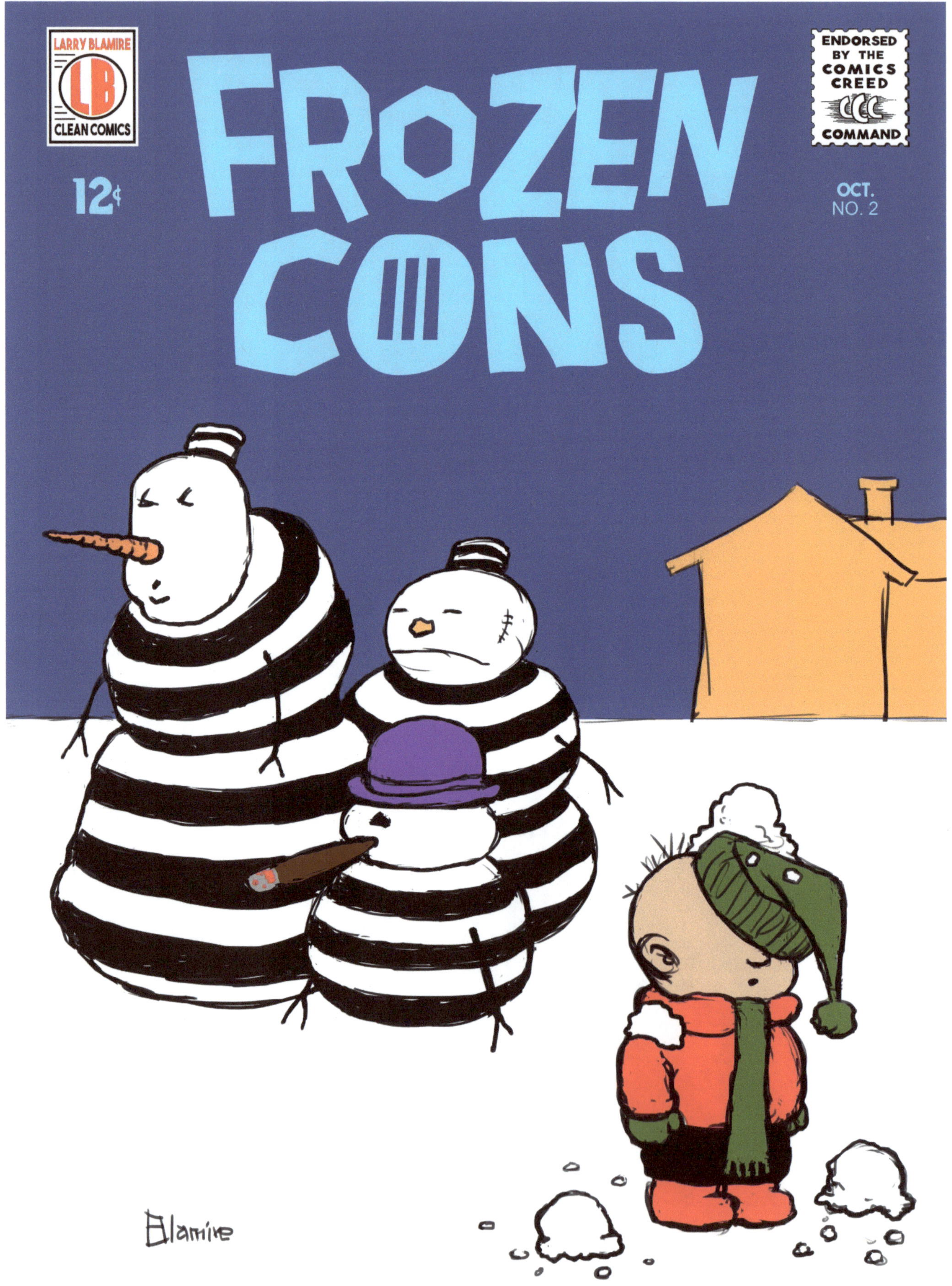
LARRY BLAMIRE
LB
CLEAN COMICS
FROZEN CONS
12¢
ENDORSED BY THE COMICS CREED
CCCC
COMMAND
OCT.
NO. 2
Blamire

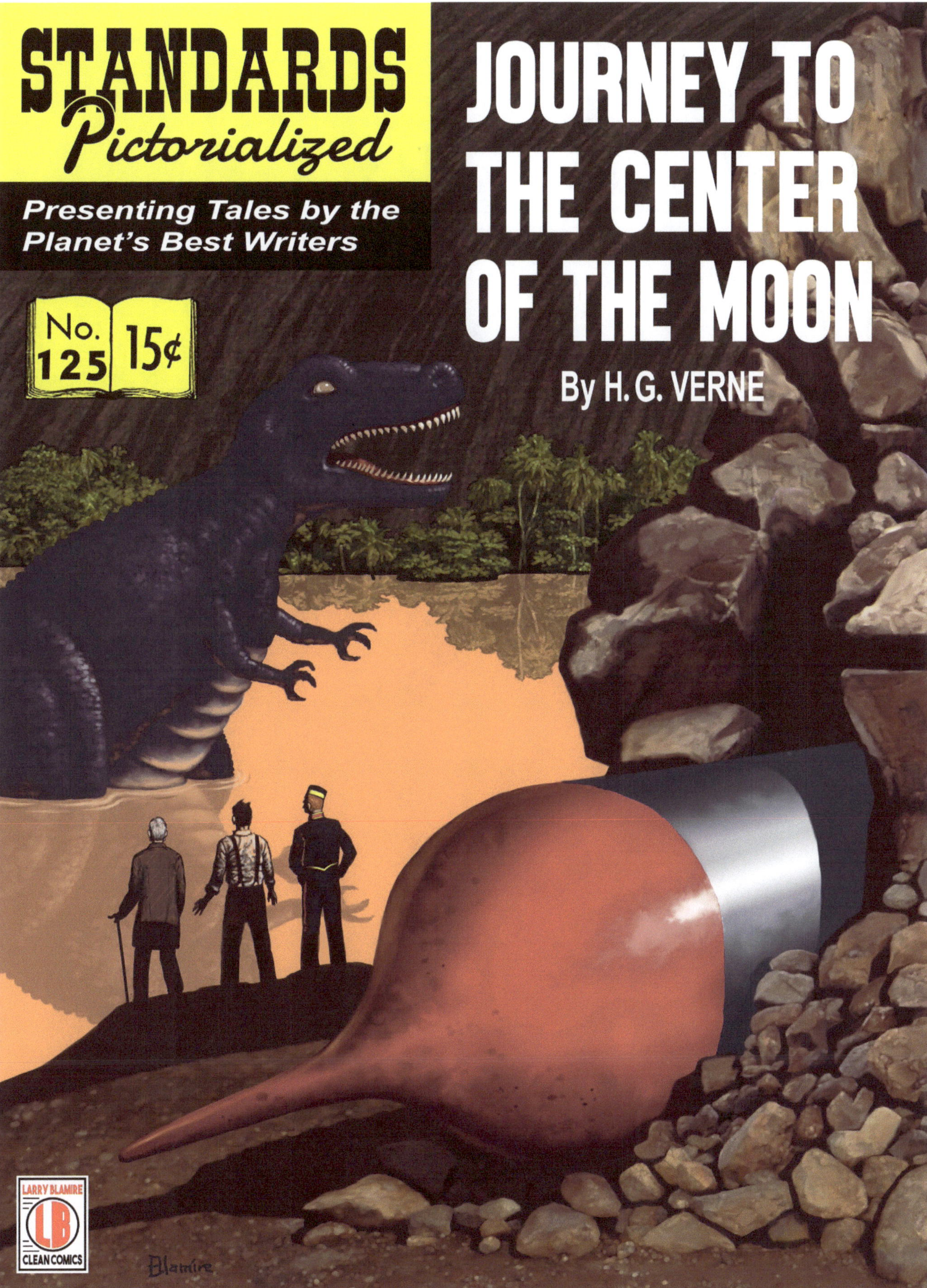
STANDARDS
Pictorialized
Presenting Tales by the
Planet's Best Writers
No. 125
15¢
JOURNEY TO
THE CENTER
OF THE MOON
By H. G. VERNE
LARRY BLAMIRE
LB
CLEAN COMICS
Blamire

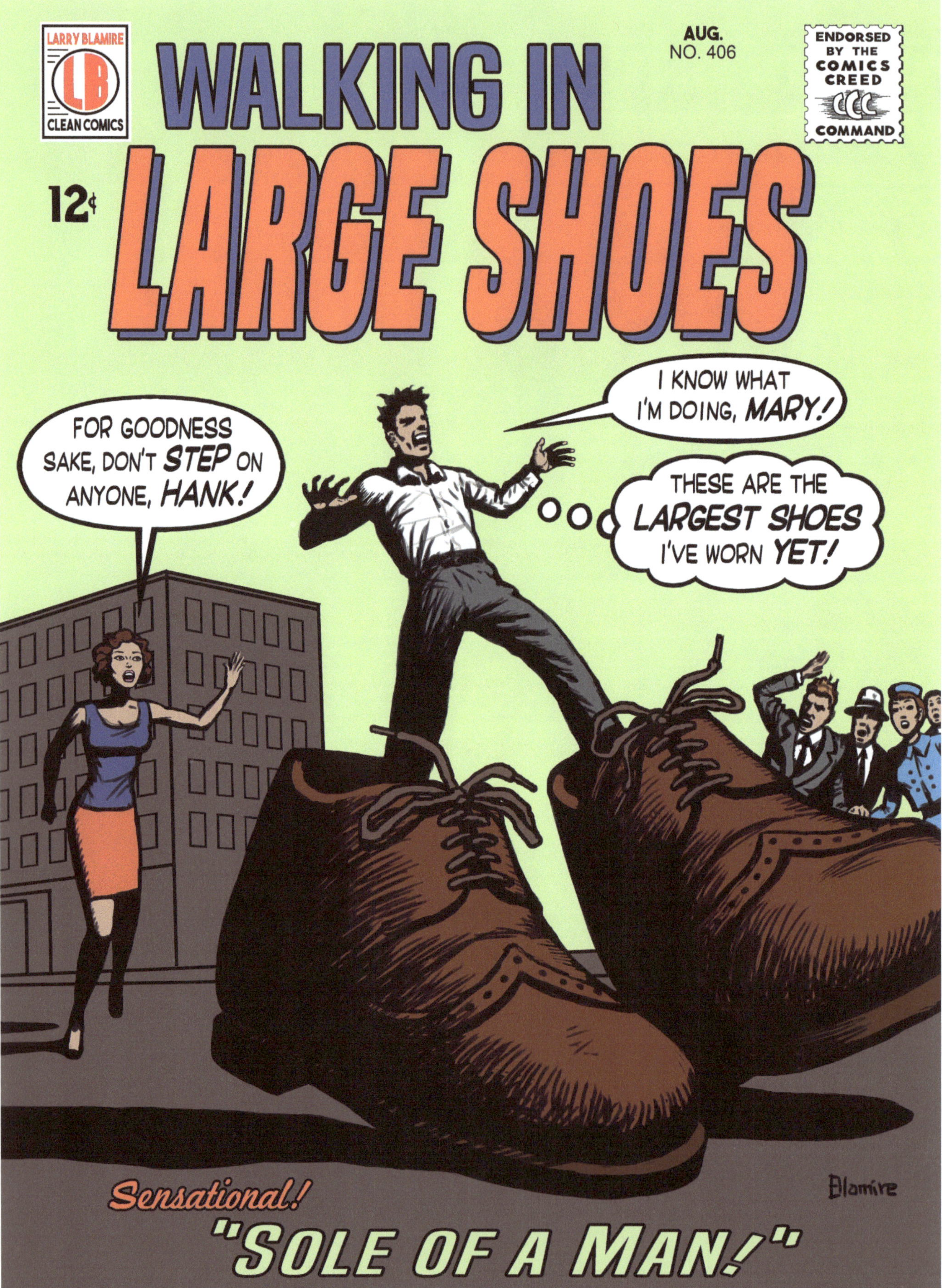
LARRY BLAMIRE
LB
CLEAN COMICS
WALKING IN
LARGE SHOES
AUG.
NO. 406
ENDORSED BY THE COMICS CREED
CCC
COMMAND
12¢
FOR GOODNESS SAKE, DON'T STEP ON ANYONE, HANK!
I KNOW WHAT I'M DOING, MARY!
THESE ARE THE LARGEST SHOES I'VE WORN YET!
Blamire
Sensational!
"SOLE OF A MAN!"

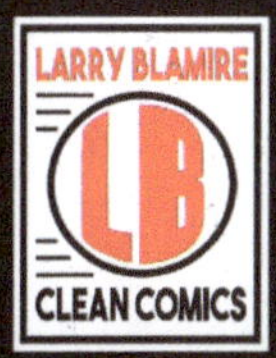

12¢

MAY
NO. 14

ENDORSED BY THE COMICS CREED CCC COMMAND

SPIRIT GUM

THE GHOST OF SOME *ALREADY CHEWED GUM!* IT'S WARNING ME! AND IT KNOWS MY ***NAME!***

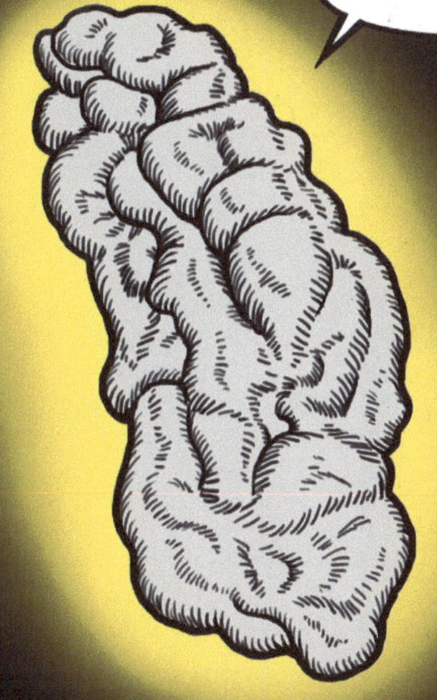

YOUR AUNT MEANS TO KILL YOU....

Incredible!

"WHEN FLAVOR DIES!"

Blamire

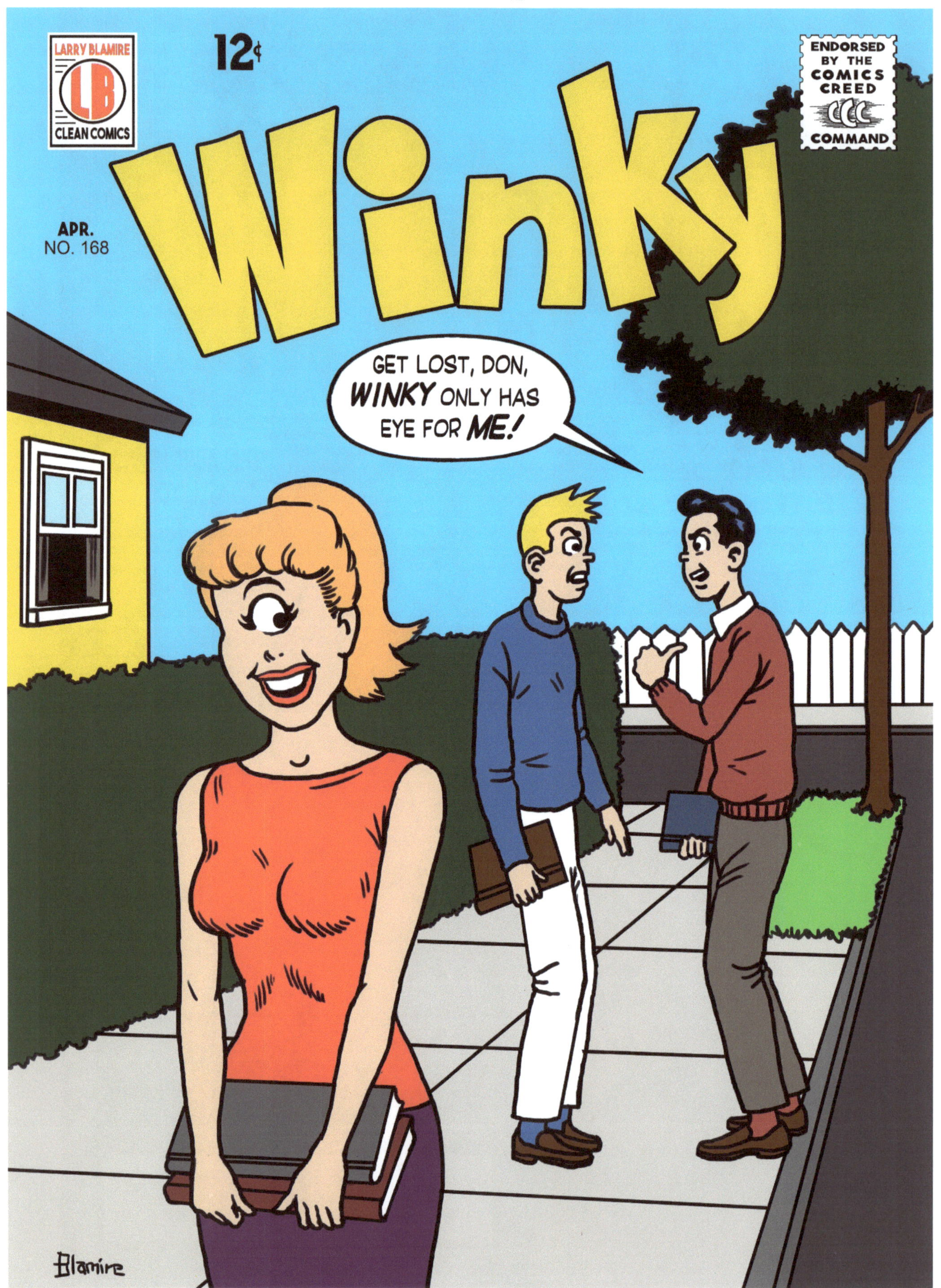
LARRY BLAMIRE
LB
CLEAN COMICS
12¢
ENDORSED BY THE COMICS CREED
CCC
COMMAND
Winky
APR.
NO. 168
GET LOST, DON, WINKY ONLY HAS EYE FOR ME!
Blamire

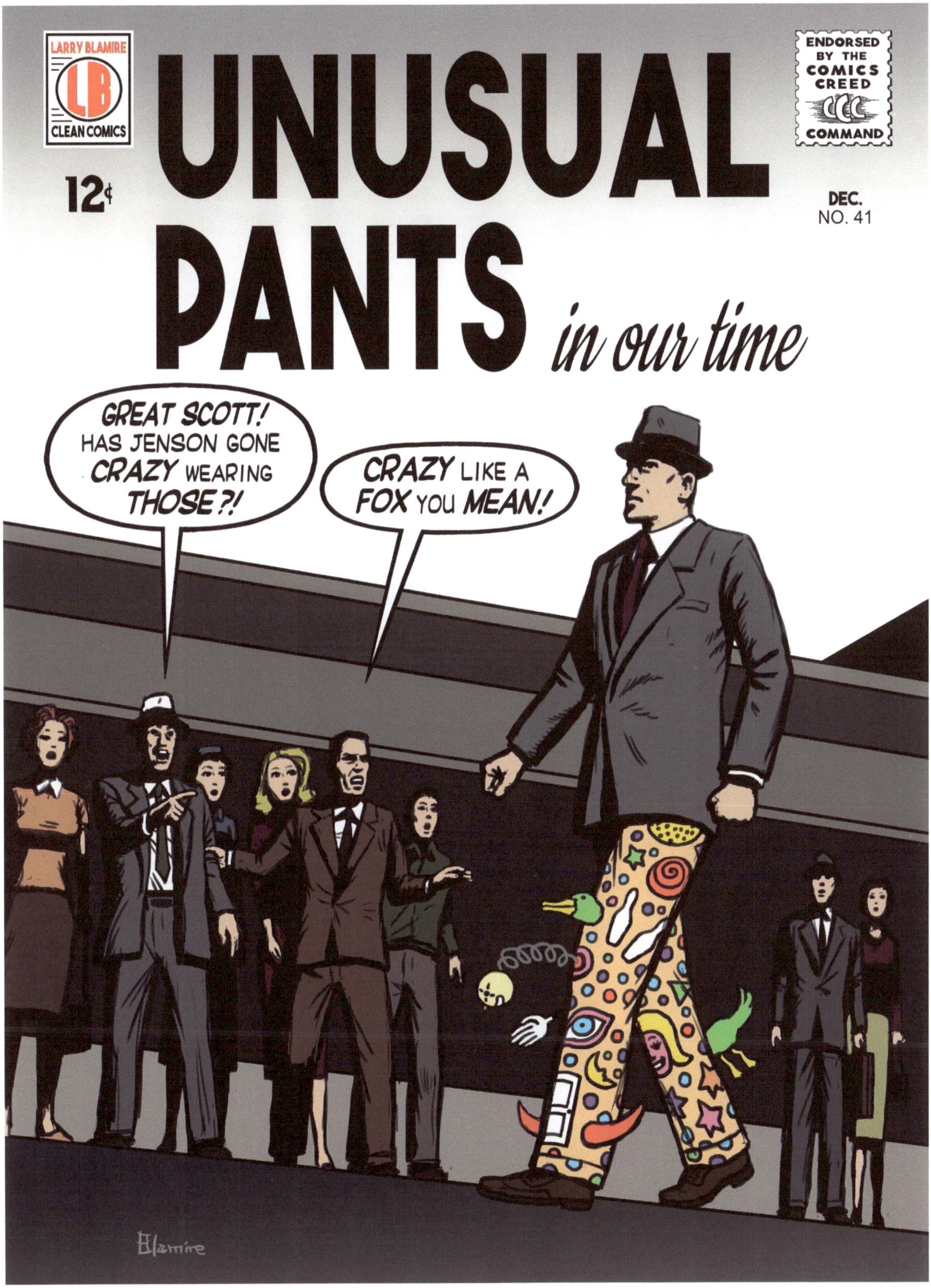

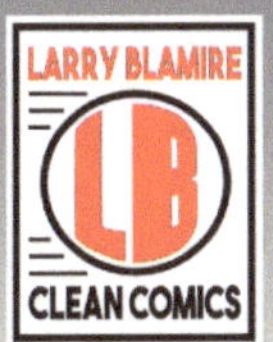
LARRY BLAMIRE
LB
CLEAN COMICS

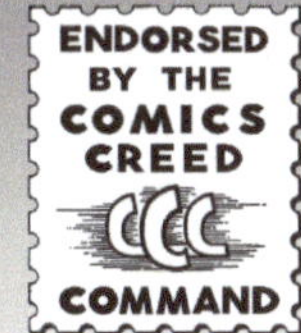
ENDORSED BY THE COMICS CREED
CCC
COMMAND

12¢
UNUSUAL PANTS in our time
DEC.
NO. 41
GREAT SCOTT! HAS JENSON GONE CRAZY WEARING THOSE?!
CRAZY LIKE A FOX YOU MEAN!
Blamire

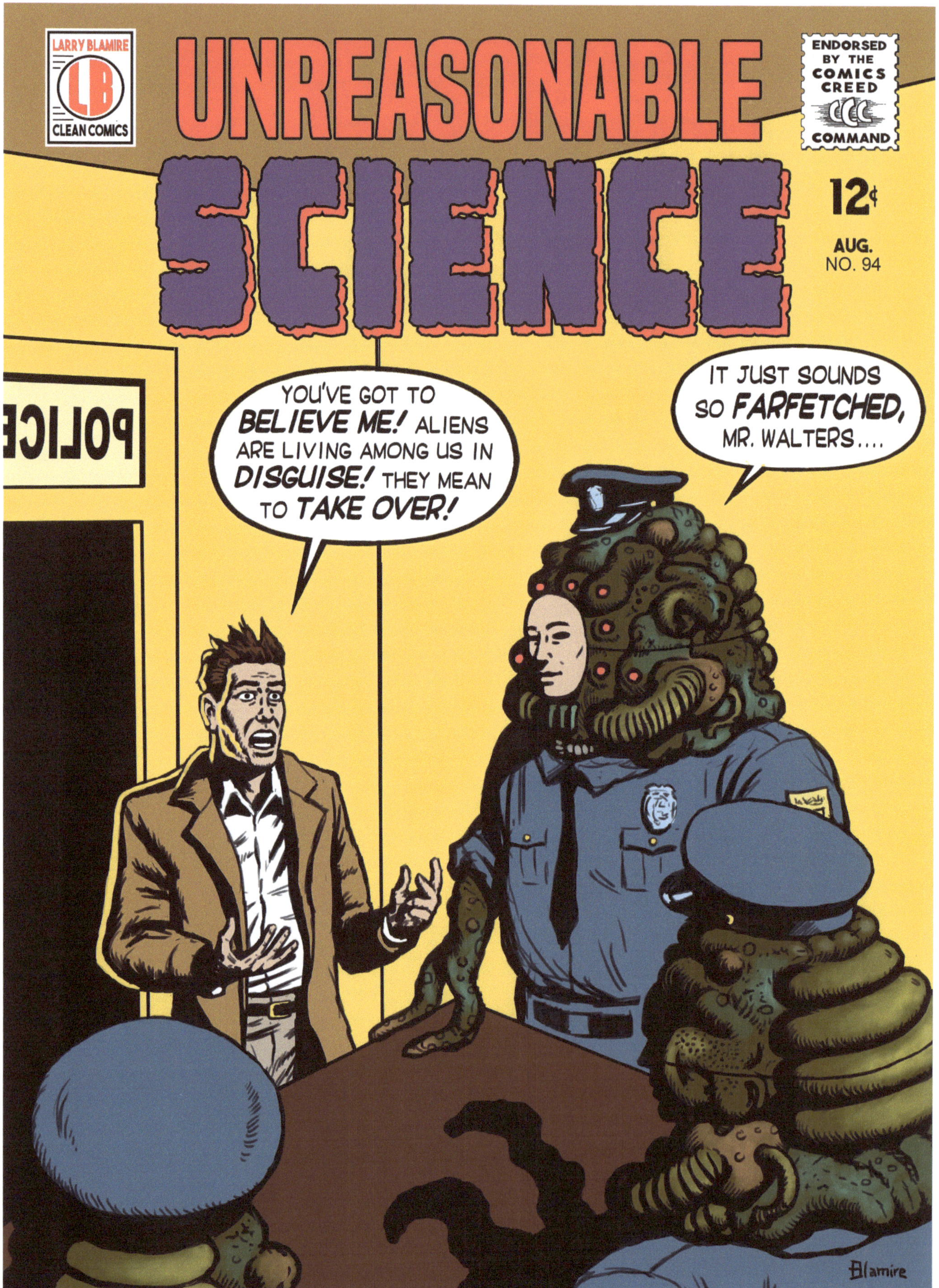
LARRY BLAMIRE
LB
CLEAN COMICS
UNREASONABLE
SCIENCE
ENDORSED BY THE COMICS CREED COMMAND
12¢
AUG.
NO. 94
POLICE
YOU'VE GOT TO BELIEVE ME! ALIENS ARE LIVING AMONG US IN DISGUISE! THEY MEAN TO TAKE OVER!
IT JUST SOUNDS SO FARFETCHED, MR. WALTERS....
Blamire

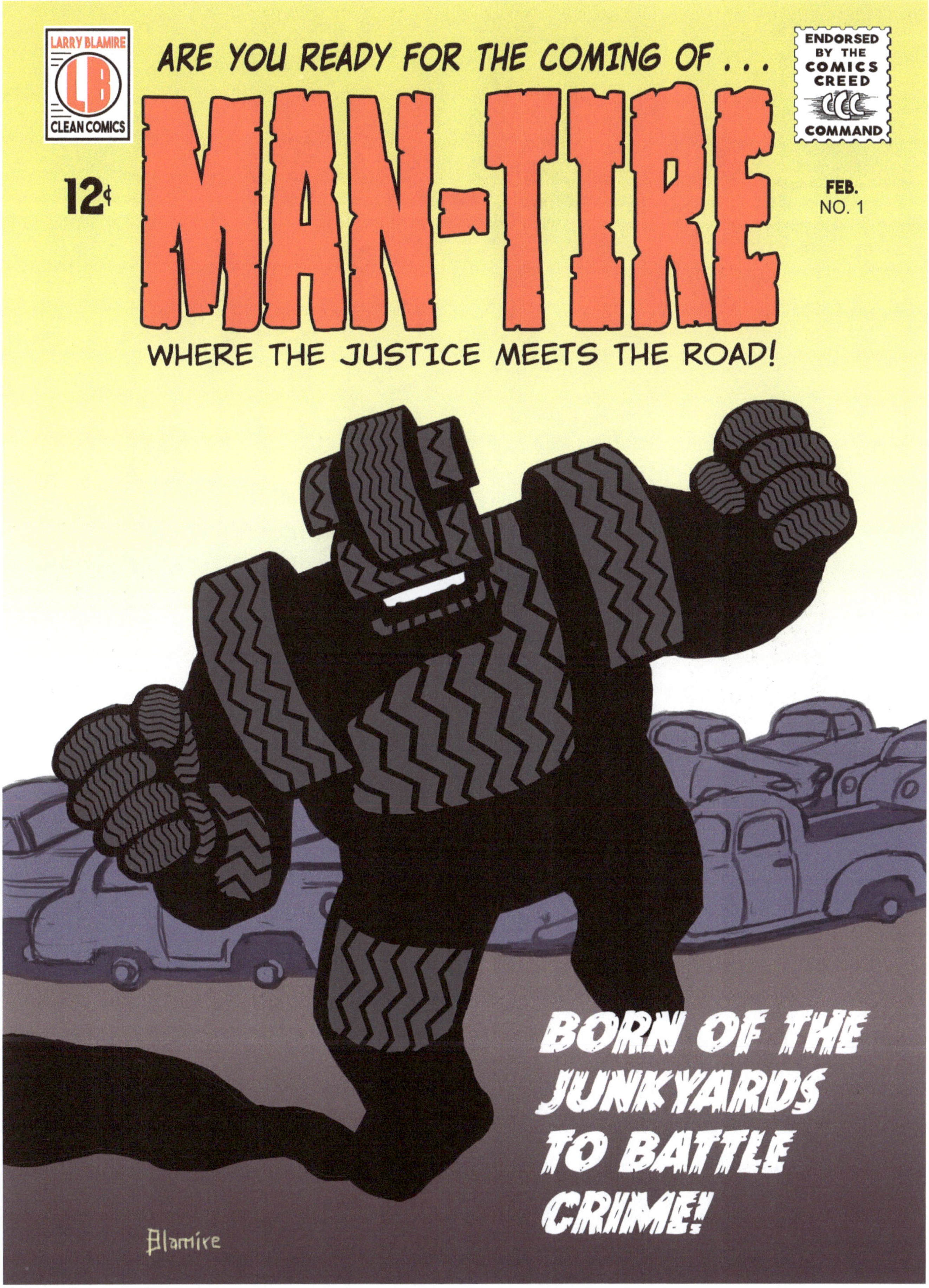

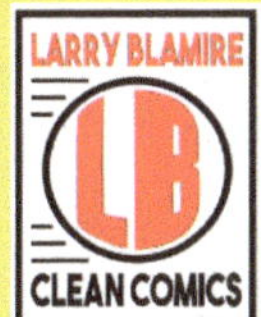
LARRY BLAMIRE
LB
CLEAN COMICS
ARE YOU READY FOR THE COMING OF . . .
ENDORSED BY THE COMICS CREED
CCC
COMMAND
12¢
MAN-TIRE
FEB.
NO. 1
WHERE THE JUSTICE MEETS THE ROAD!
BORN OF THE JUNKYARDS TO BATTLE CRIME!
Blamire

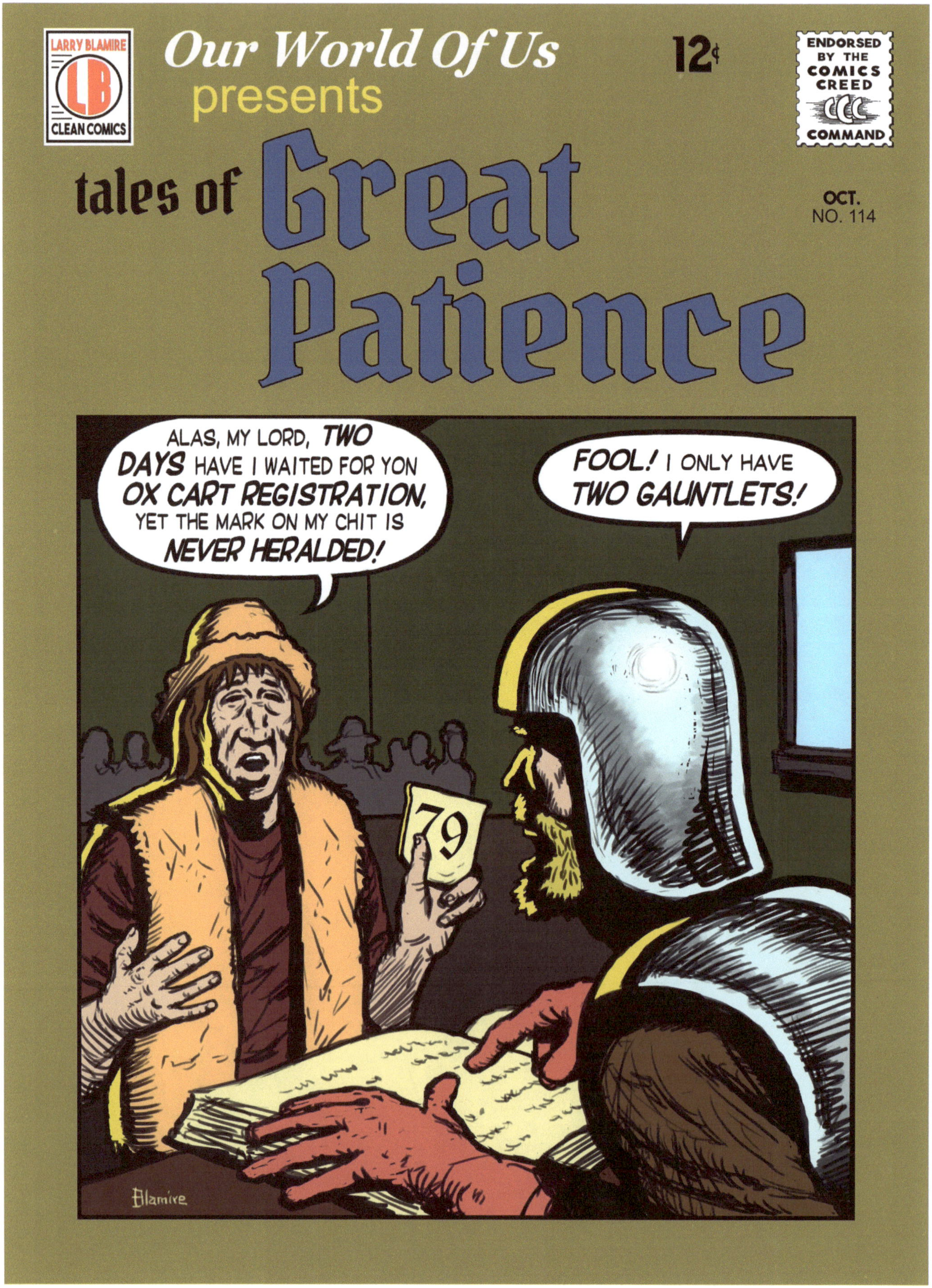

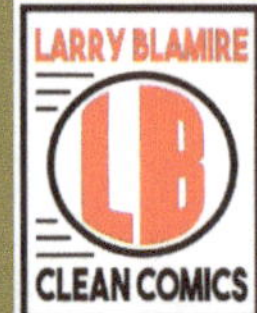

Our World Of Us

presents

12¢

ENDORSED BY THE COMICS CREED

CCCC

COMMAND

tales of Great Patience

OCT.
NO. 114

ALAS, MY LORD, **TWO DAYS** HAVE I WAITED FOR YON **OX CART REGISTRATION,** YET THE MARK ON MY CHIT IS **NEVER HERALDED!**

FOOL! I ONLY HAVE **TWO GAUNTLETS!**

79

Blamire

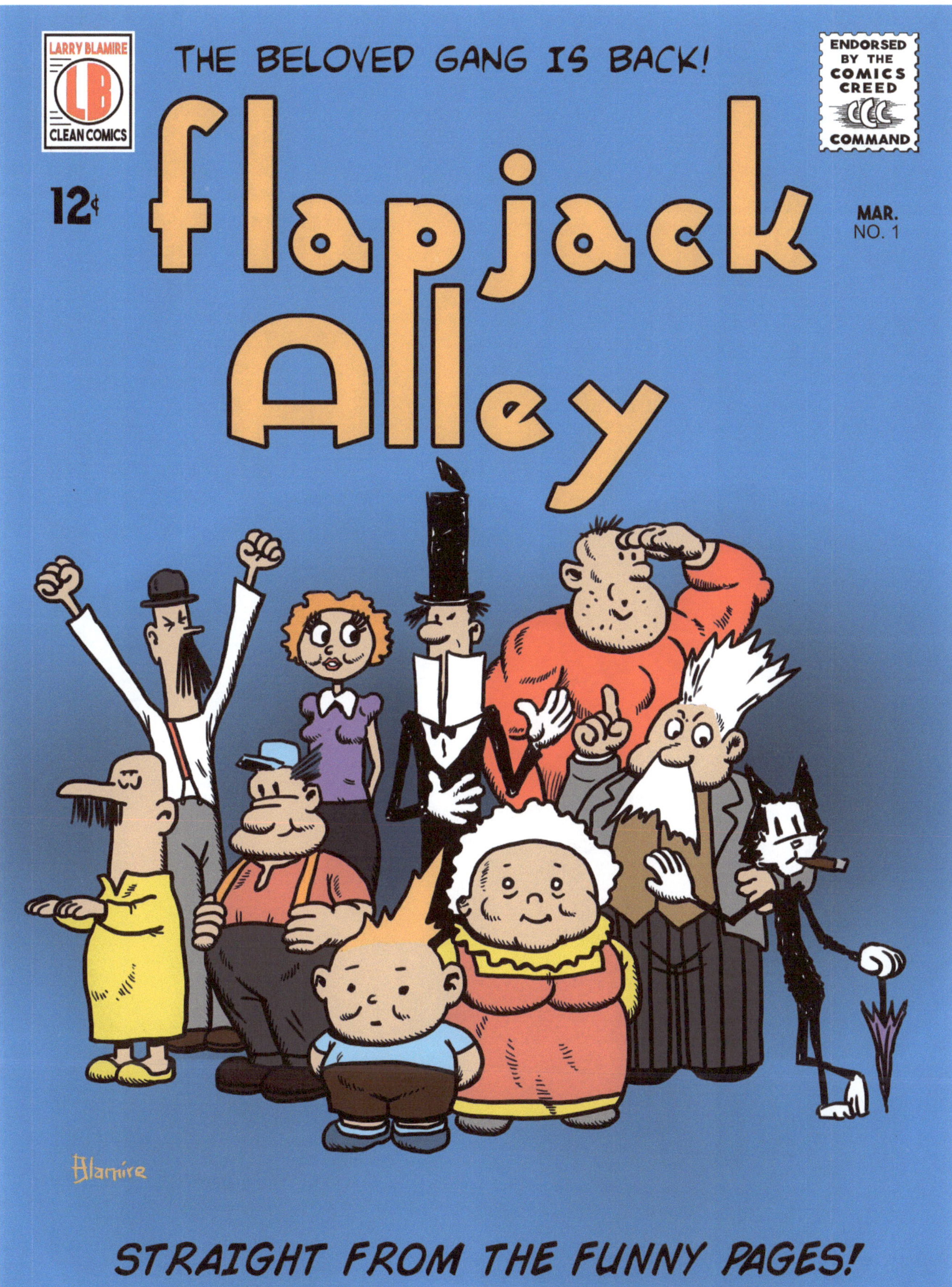
LARRY BLAMIRE
LB
CLEAN COMICS
THE BELOVED GANG IS BACK!
ENDORSED BY THE COMICS CREED
CCC
COMMAND
12¢
flapjack Alley
MAR.
NO. 1
Blamire
STRAIGHT FROM THE FUNNY PAGES!

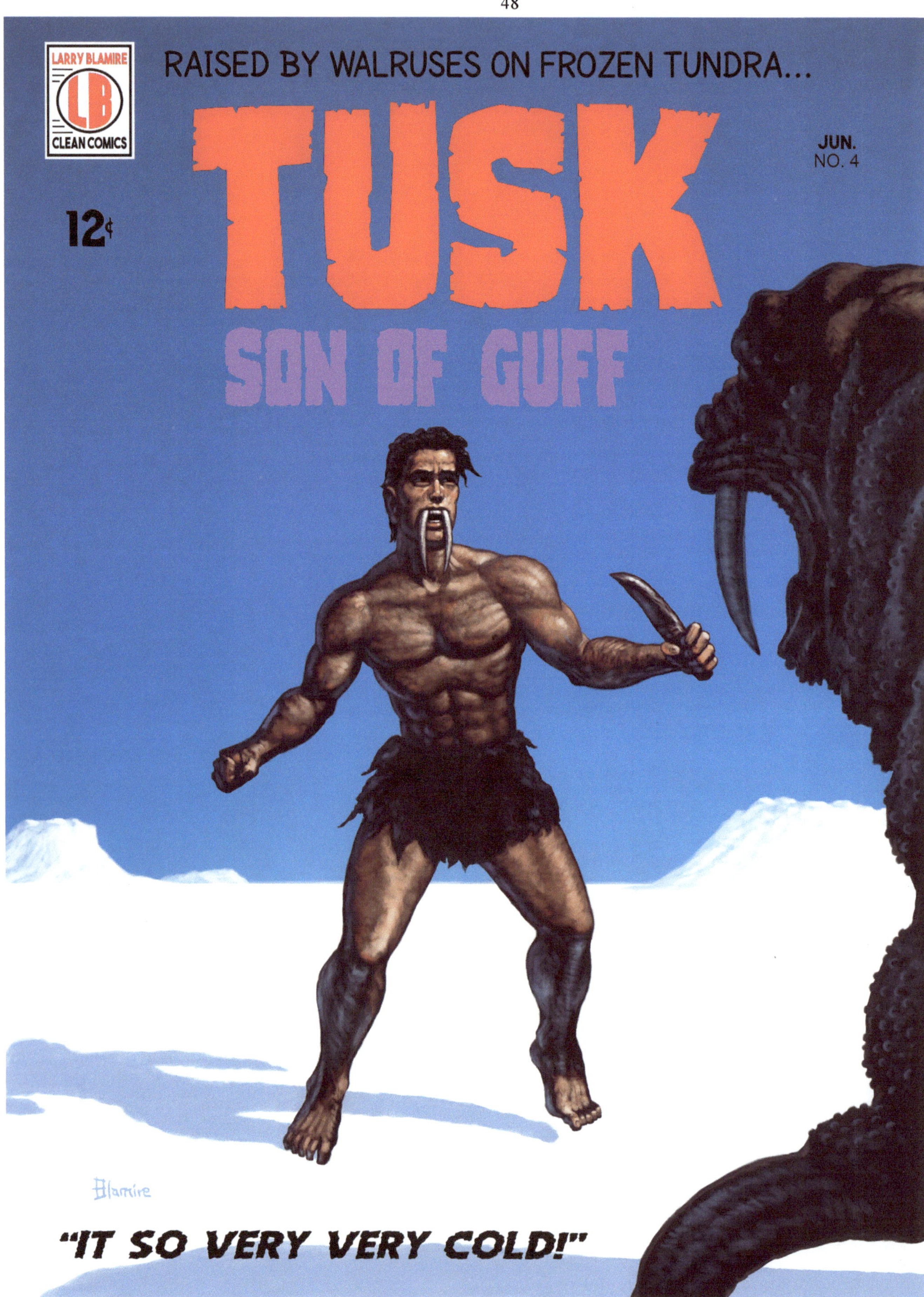
LARRY BLAMIRE
LB
CLEAN COMICS
RAISED BY WALRUSES ON FROZEN TUNDRA...
TUSK
SON OF GUFF
JUN.
NO. 4
12¢
Blamire
"IT SO VERY VERY COLD!"

LARRY BLAMIRE
LB
CLEAN COMICS
THAT VEXING
UNKNOWN
ENDORSED BY THE COMICS CREED
CCC
COMMAND
12¢
JAN.
NO. 213
GREAT SCOTT! THAT ALIEN BEAM! FORCING ME TO SAY GREAT SCOTT AND EXPLAIN EVERYTHING THAT'S HAPPENING TO ME!
Blamire
" The ALIENS WHO MADE PEOPLE EXPLAIN!"

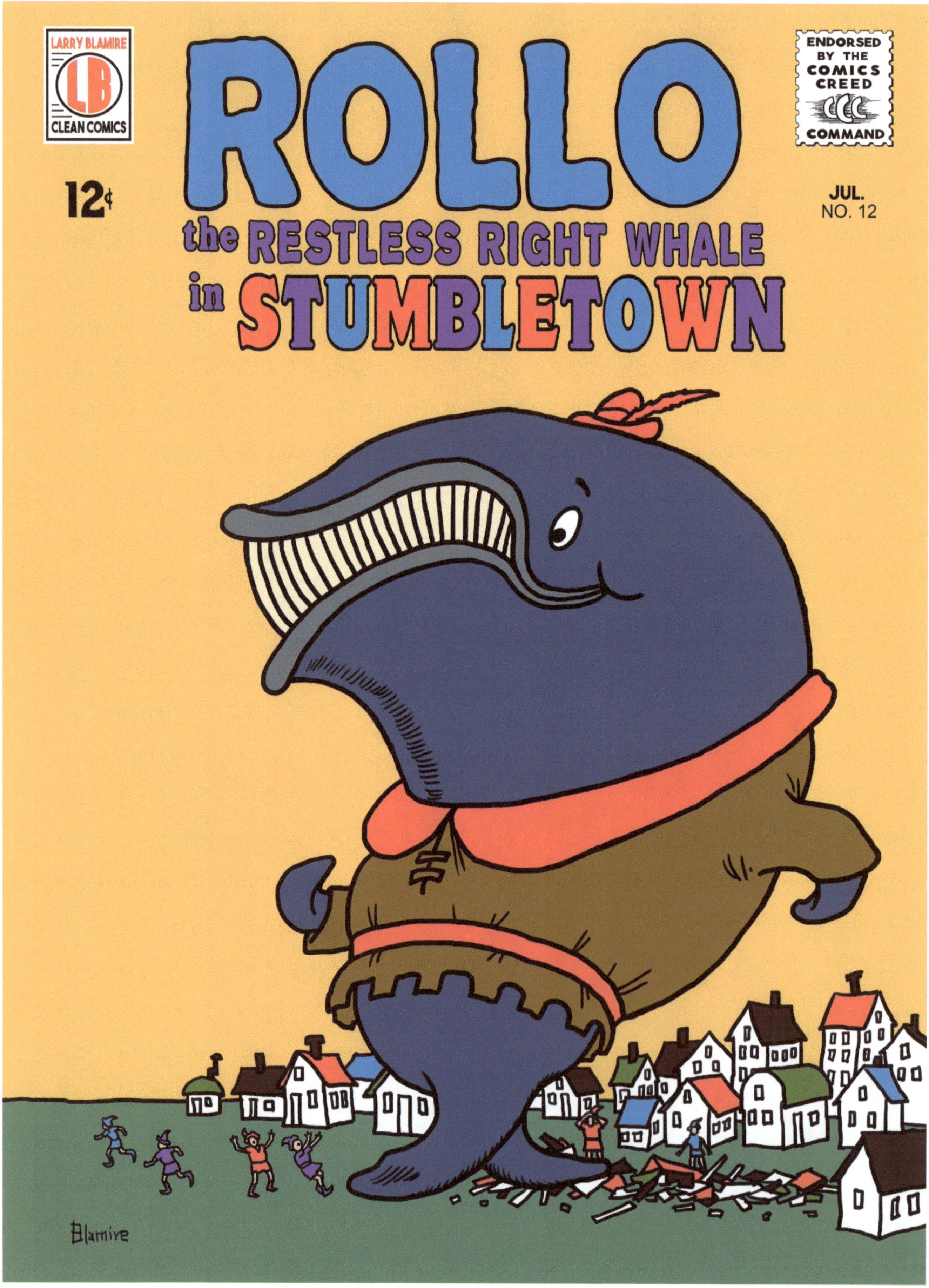

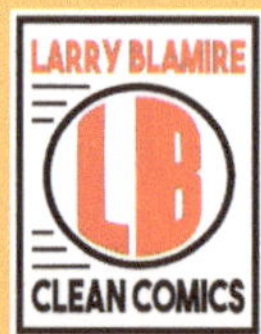

ROLLO

the RESTLESS RIGHT WHALE in STUMBLETOWN

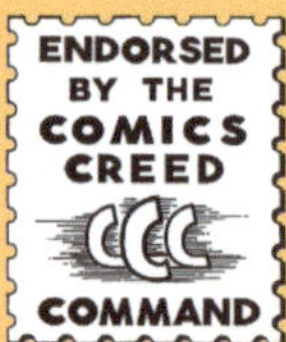

12¢

JUL.
NO. 12

Blamire

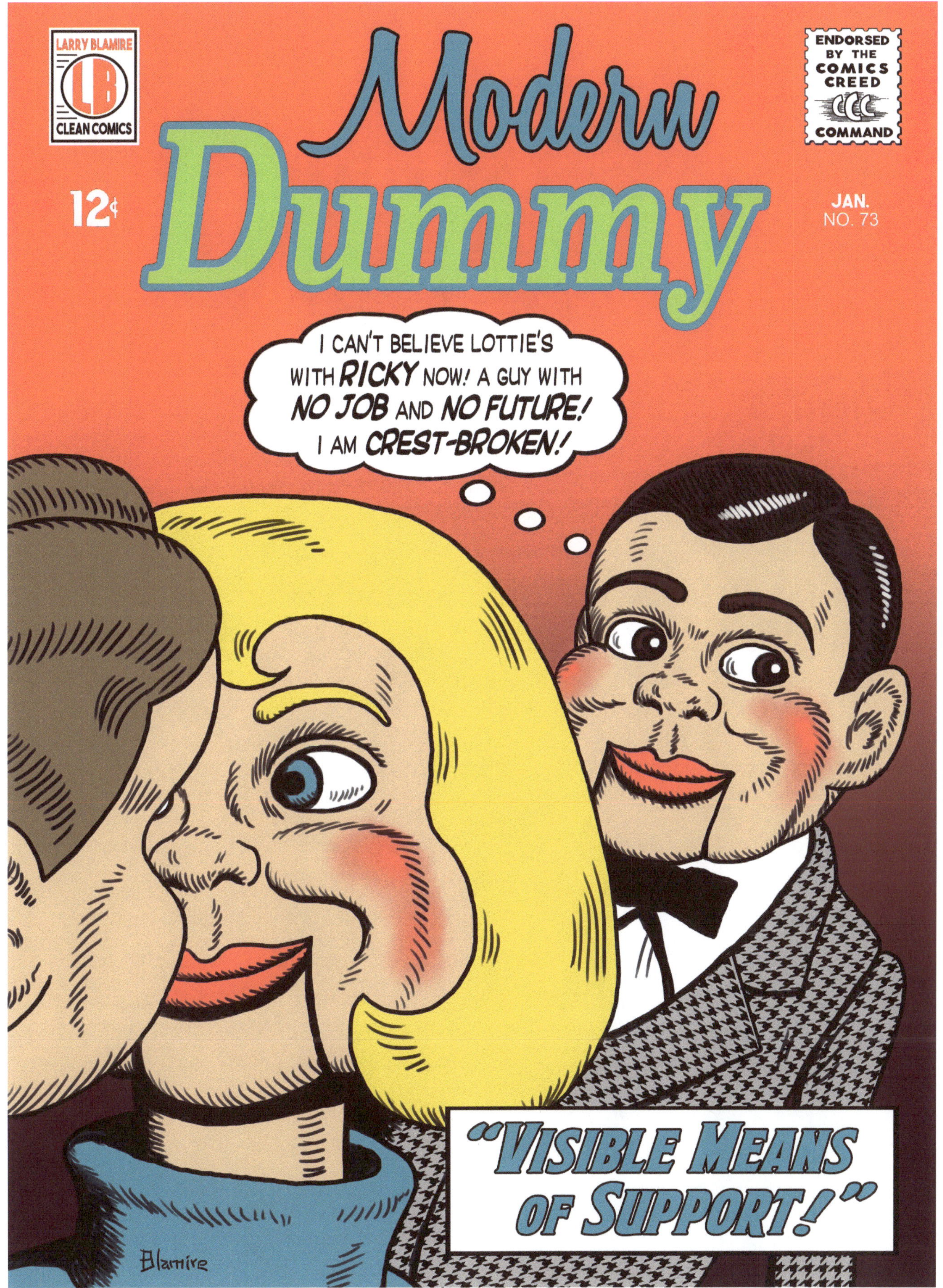
LARRY BLAMIRE
LB
CLEAN COMICS
Modern Dummy
ENDORSED BY THE COMICS CREED
CCC
COMMAND
12¢
JAN.
NO. 73
I CAN'T BELIEVE LOTTIE'S WITH RICKY NOW! A GUY WITH NO JOB AND NO FUTURE! I AM CREST-BROKEN!
"VISIBLE MEANS OF SUPPORT!"
Blamire

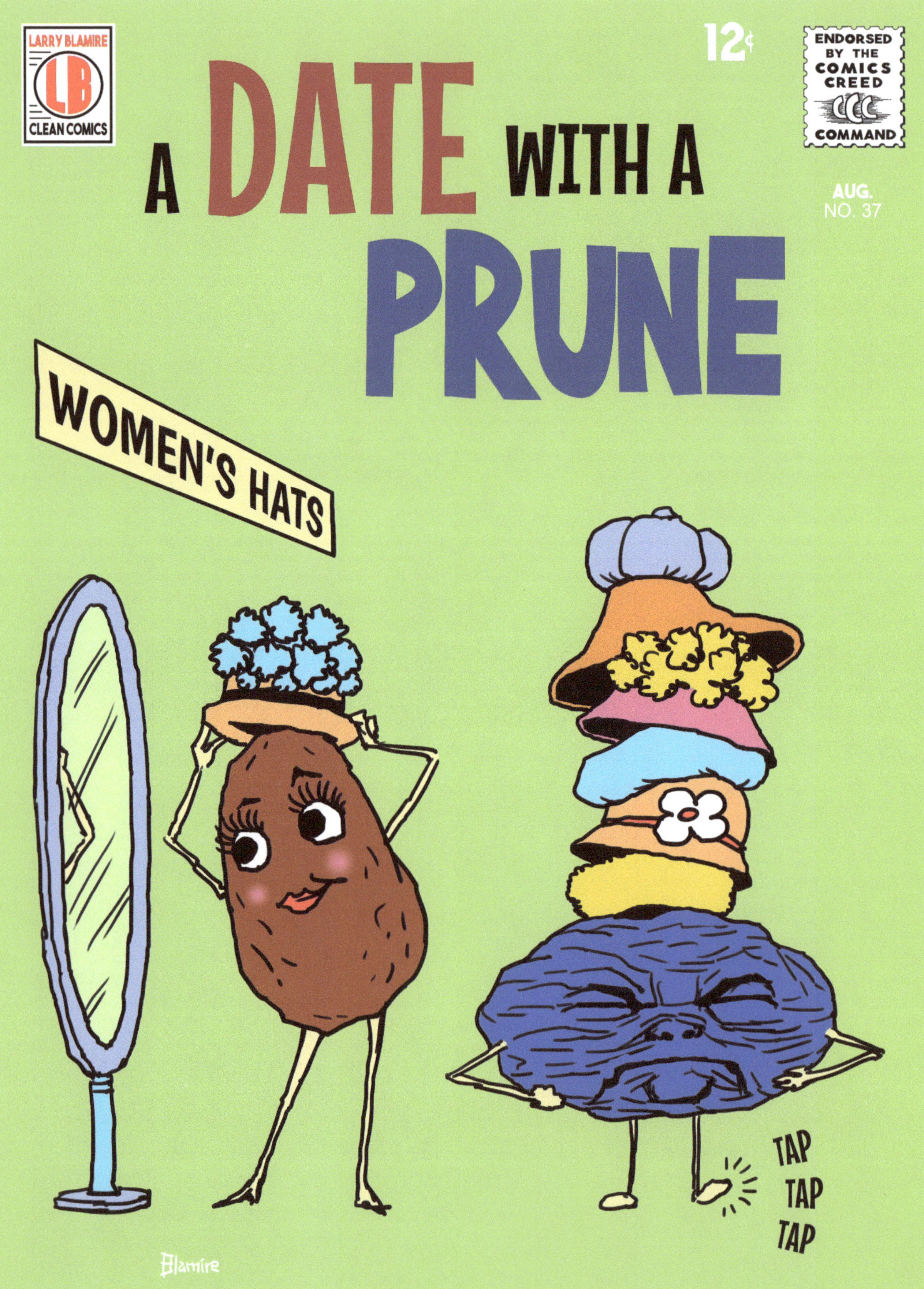
LARRY BLAMIRE
LB
CLEAN COMICS
12¢
ENDORSED BY THE COMICS CREED
CCC
COMMAND
A DATE WITH A
PRUNE
AUG.
NO. 37
WOMEN'S HATS
TAP
TAP
TAP
Blamire

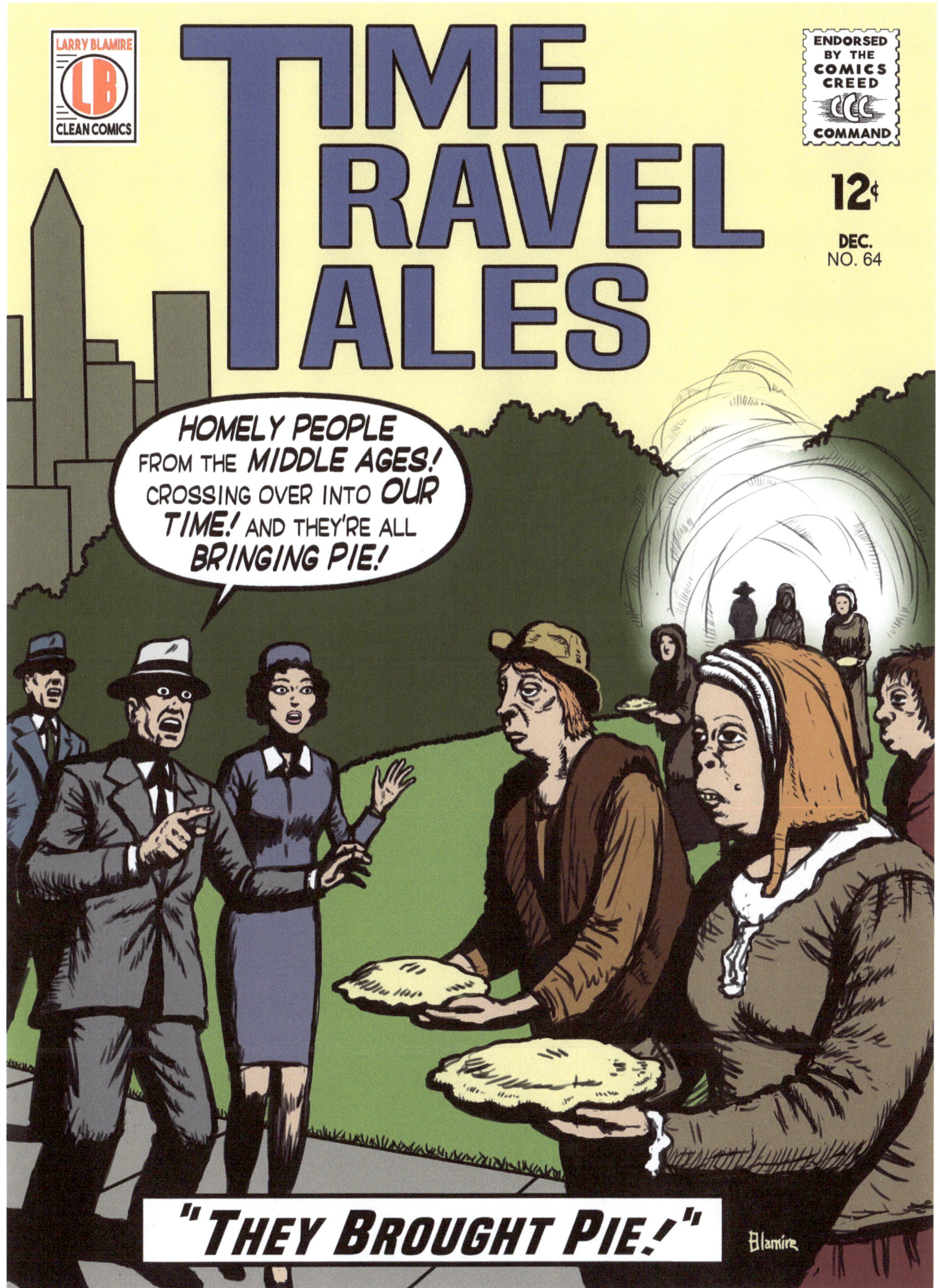
LARRY BLAMIRE
LB
CLEAN COMICS
TIME TRAVEL TALES
ENDORSED BY THE COMICS CREED CCC COMMAND
12¢
DEC.
NO. 64
HOMELY PEOPLE FROM THE MIDDLE AGES! CROSSING OVER INTO OUR TIME! AND THEY'RE ALL BRINGING PIE!
"THEY BROUGHT PIE!"
Blamire

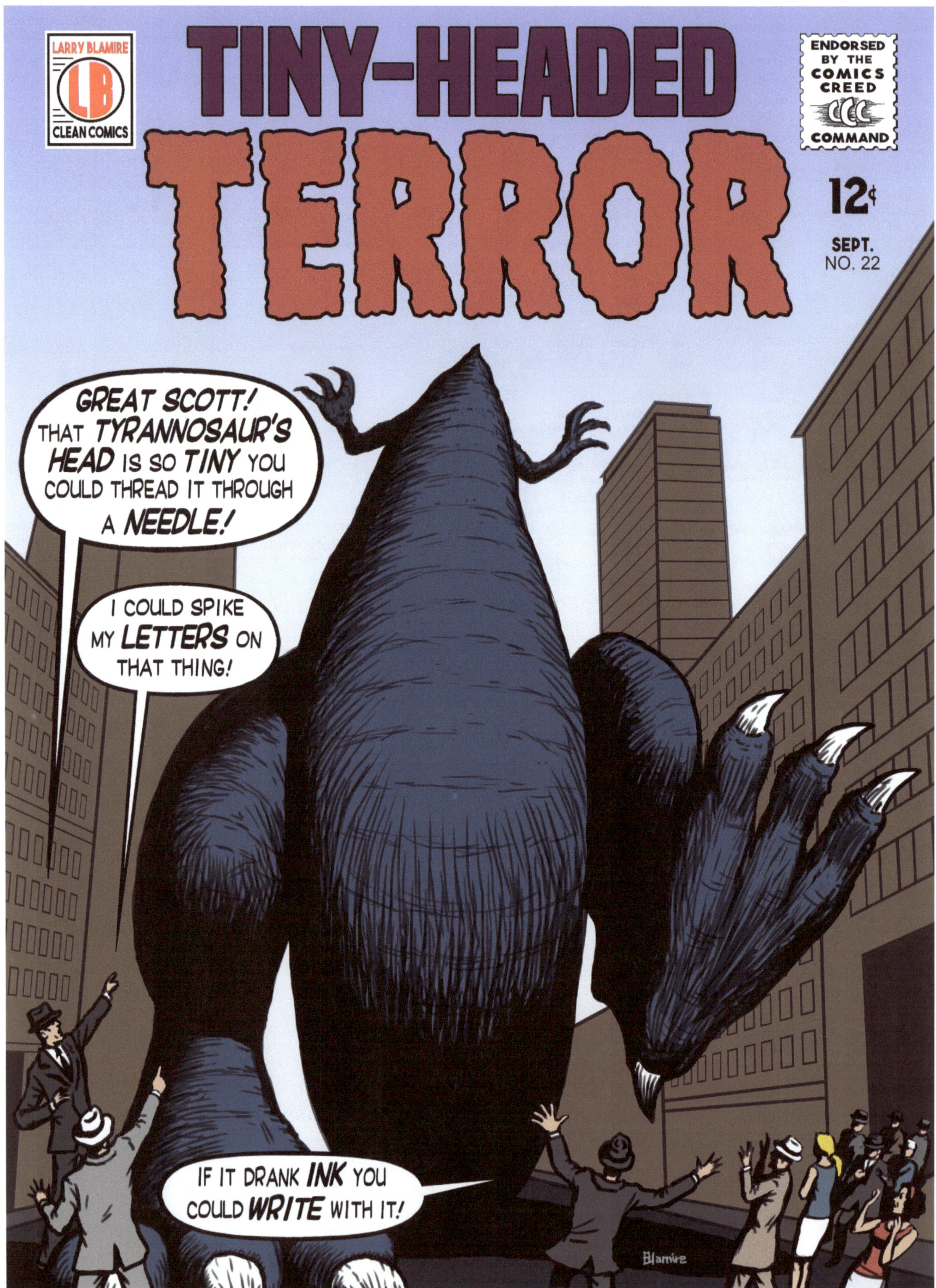
LARRY BLAMIRE
LB
CLEAN COMICS
TINY-HEADED
TERROR
ENDORSED BY THE COMICS CREED
CCC
COMMAND
12¢
SEPT.
NO. 22
GREAT SCOTT! THAT TYRANNOSAUR'S HEAD IS SO TINY YOU COULD THREAD IT THROUGH A NEEDLE!
I COULD SPIKE MY LETTERS ON THAT THING!
IF IT DRANK INK YOU COULD WRITE WITH IT!
Blamire

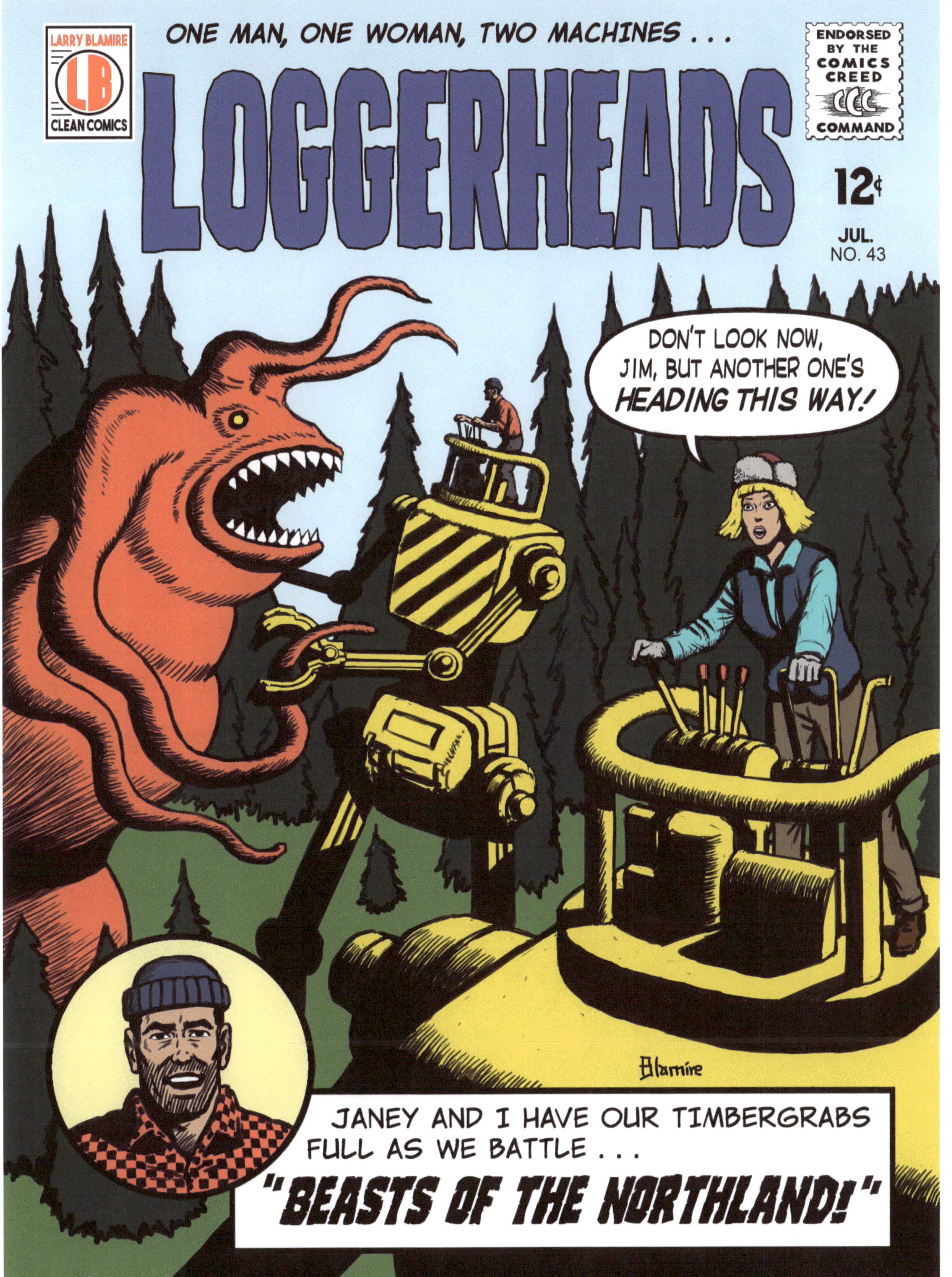
LARRY BLAMIRE
LB
CLEAN COMICS
ONE MAN, ONE WOMAN, TWO MACHINES . . .
LOGGERHEADS
ENDORSED BY THE COMICS CREED
CCC
COMMAND
12¢
JUL.
NO. 43
DON'T LOOK NOW, JIM, BUT ANOTHER ONE'S HEADING THIS WAY!
Blamire
JANEY AND I HAVE OUR TIMBERGRABS FULL AS WE BATTLE . . .
"BEASTS OF THE NORTHLAND!"

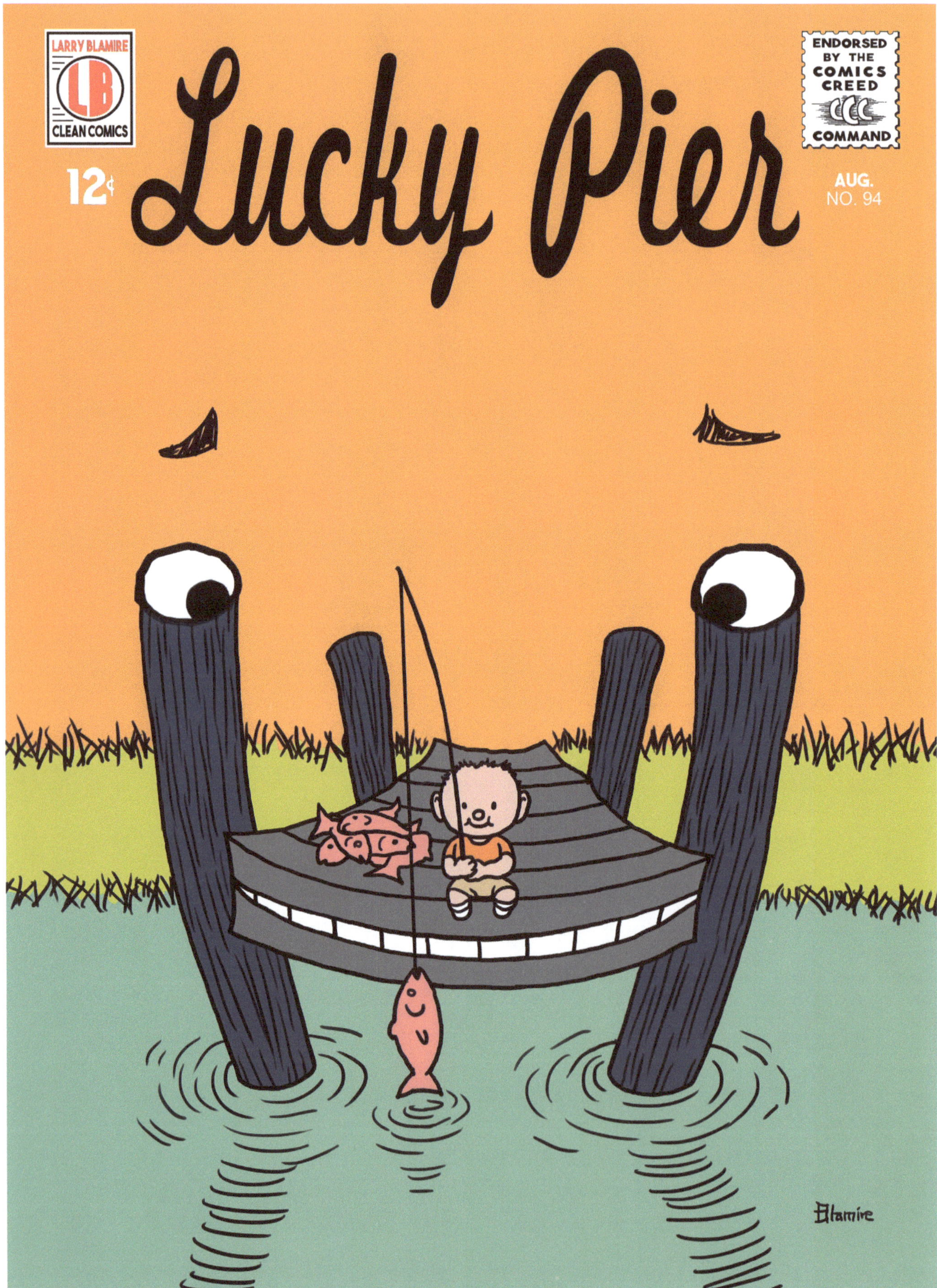
LARRY BLAMIRE
LB
CLEAN COMICS
12¢
Lucky Pier
ENDORSED BY THE COMICS CREED
CCC
COMMAND
AUG.
NO. 94
Blamire

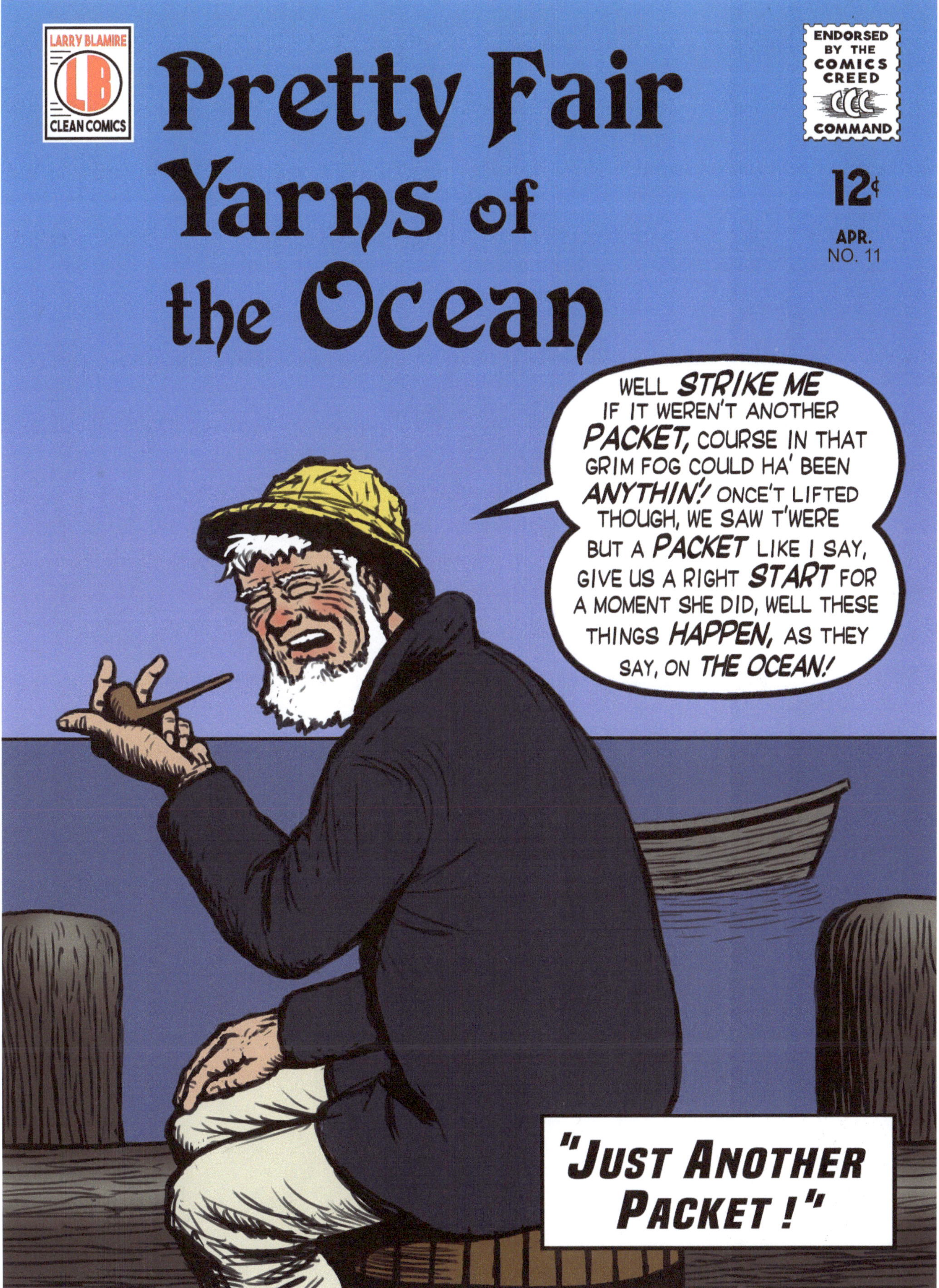
LARRY BLAMIRE
LB
CLEAN COMICS
Pretty Fair Yarns of the Ocean
ENDORSED BY THE COMICS CREED
CCC
COMMAND
12¢
APR.
NO. 11
WELL STRIKE ME IF IT WEREN'T ANOTHER PACKET, COURSE IN THAT GRIM FOG COULD HA' BEEN ANYTHIN'! ONCE'T LIFTED THOUGH, WE SAW T'WERE BUT A PACKET LIKE I SAY, GIVE US A RIGHT START FOR A MOMENT SHE DID, WELL THESE THINGS HAPPEN, AS THEY SAY, ON THE OCEAN!
"JUST ANOTHER PACKET!"

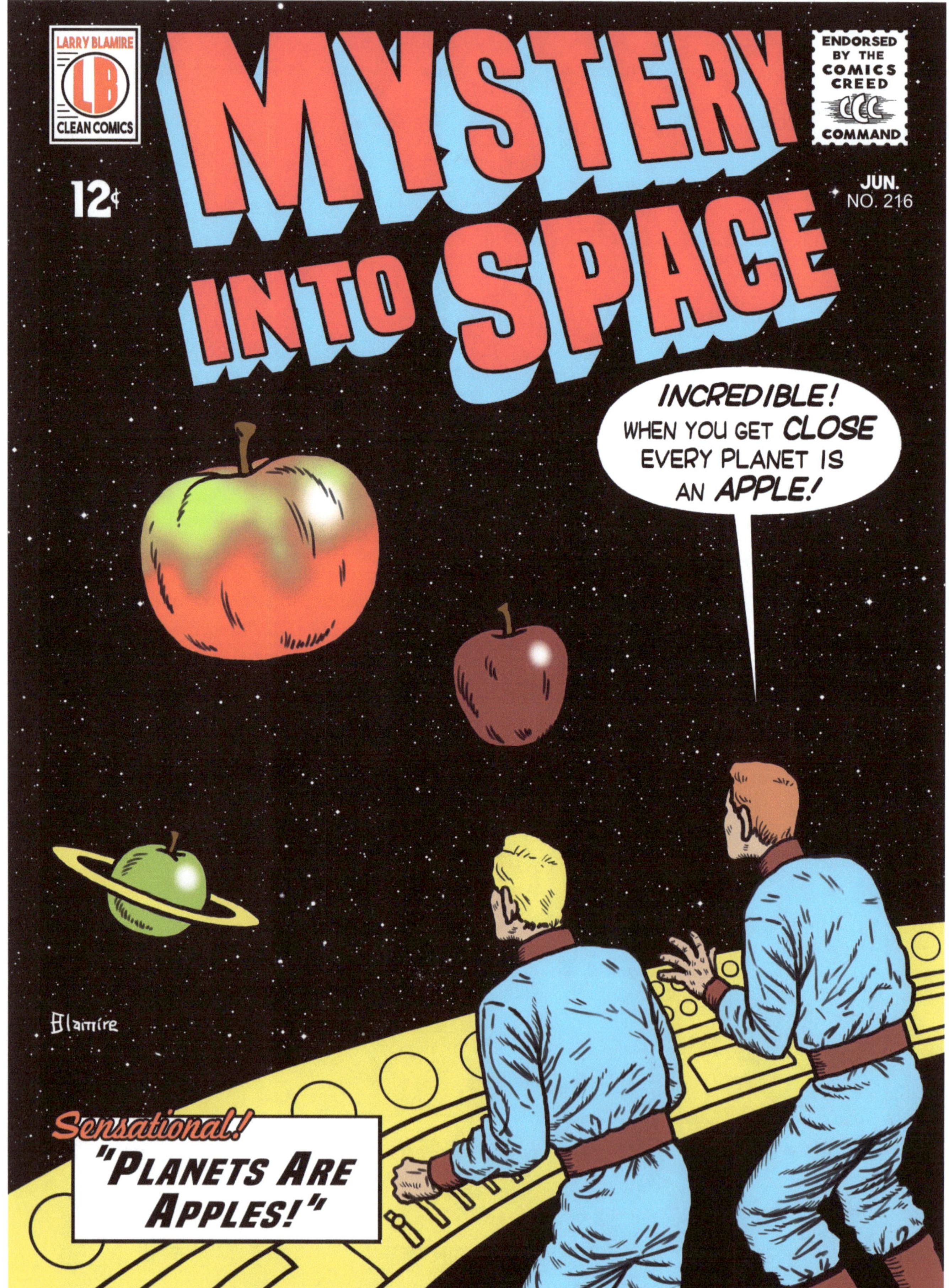
LARRY BLAMIRE
LB
CLEAN COMICS
MYSTERY INTO SPACE
ENDORSED BY THE COMICS CREED
CCC
COMMAND
12¢
JUN.
NO. 216
INCREDIBLE! WHEN YOU GET CLOSE EVERY PLANET IS AN APPLE!
Blamire
Sensational!
"PLANETS ARE APPLES!"

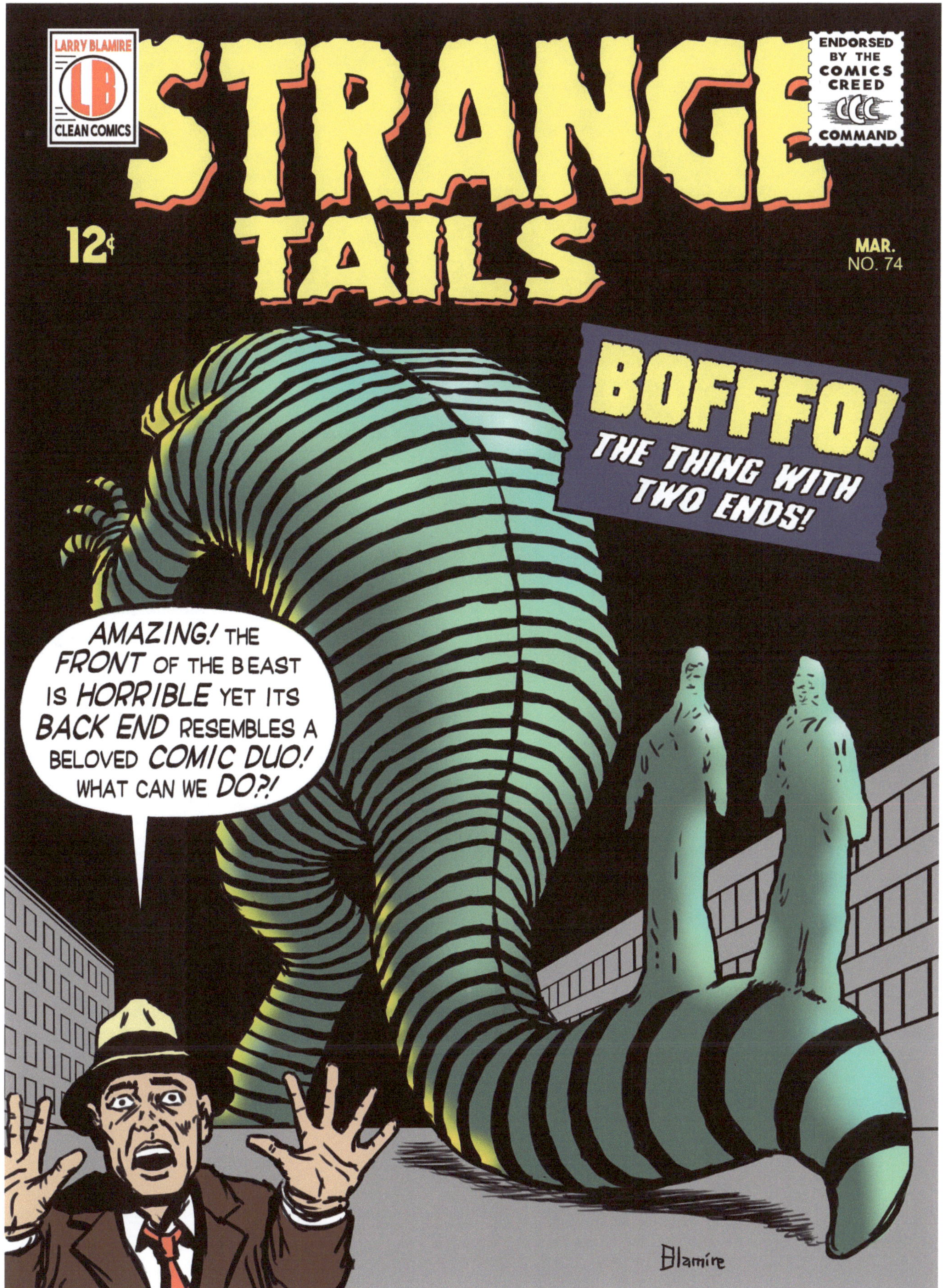
LARRY BLAMIRE
LB
CLEAN COMICS
STRANGE TAILS
ENDORSED BY THE COMICS CREED
CCCC
COMMAND
12¢
MAR.
NO. 74
BOFFFO!
THE THING WITH TWO ENDS!
AMAZING! THE FRONT OF THE BEAST IS HORRIBLE YET ITS BACK END RESEMBLES A BELOVED COMIC DUO! WHAT CAN WE DO?!
Blamire

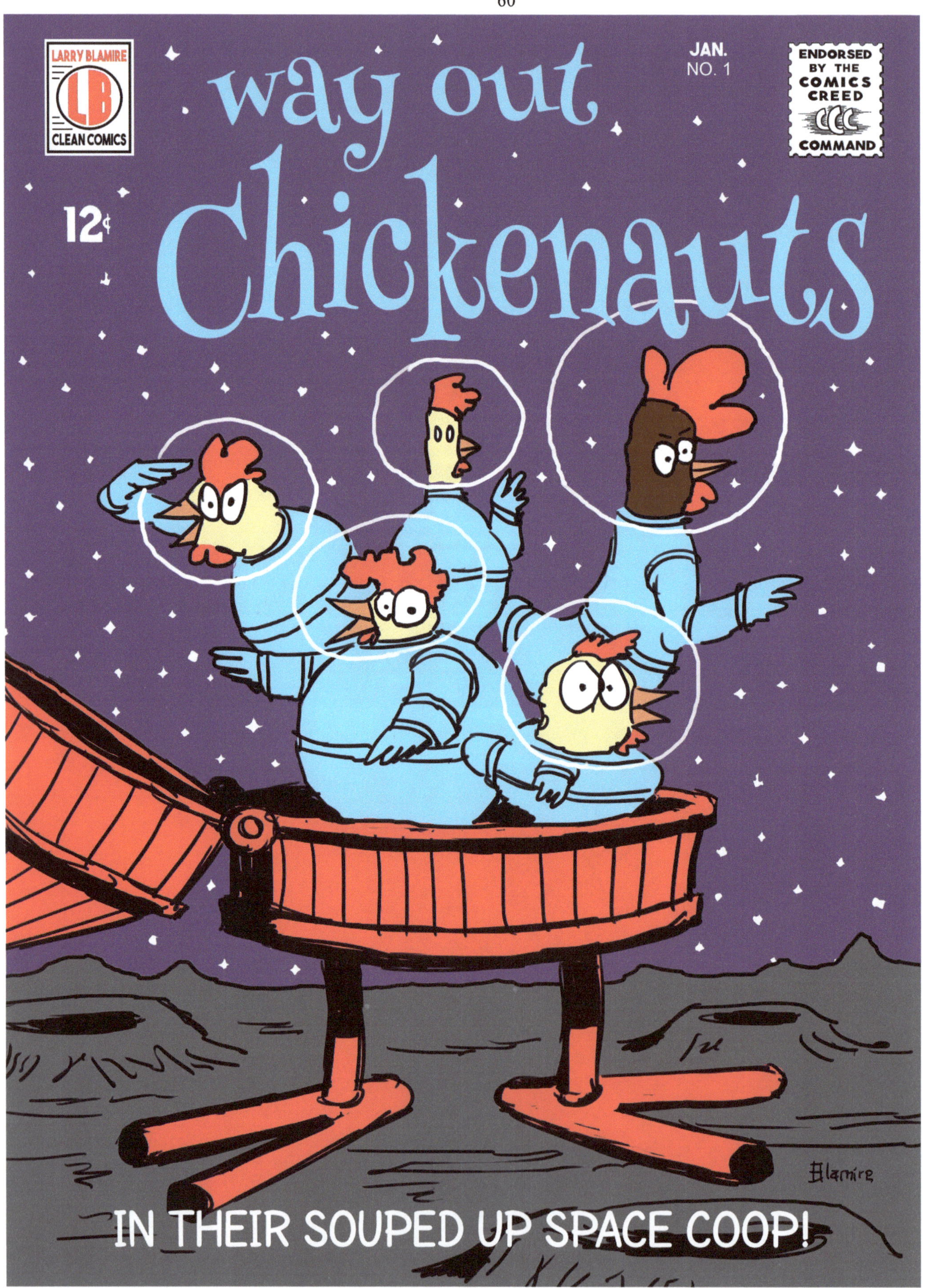
LARRY BLAMIRE
LB
CLEAN COMICS
JAN.
NO. 1
ENDORSED BY THE COMICS CREED
CCC
COMMAND
way out
Chickenauts
12¢
Blamire
IN THEIR SOUPED UP SPACE COOP!

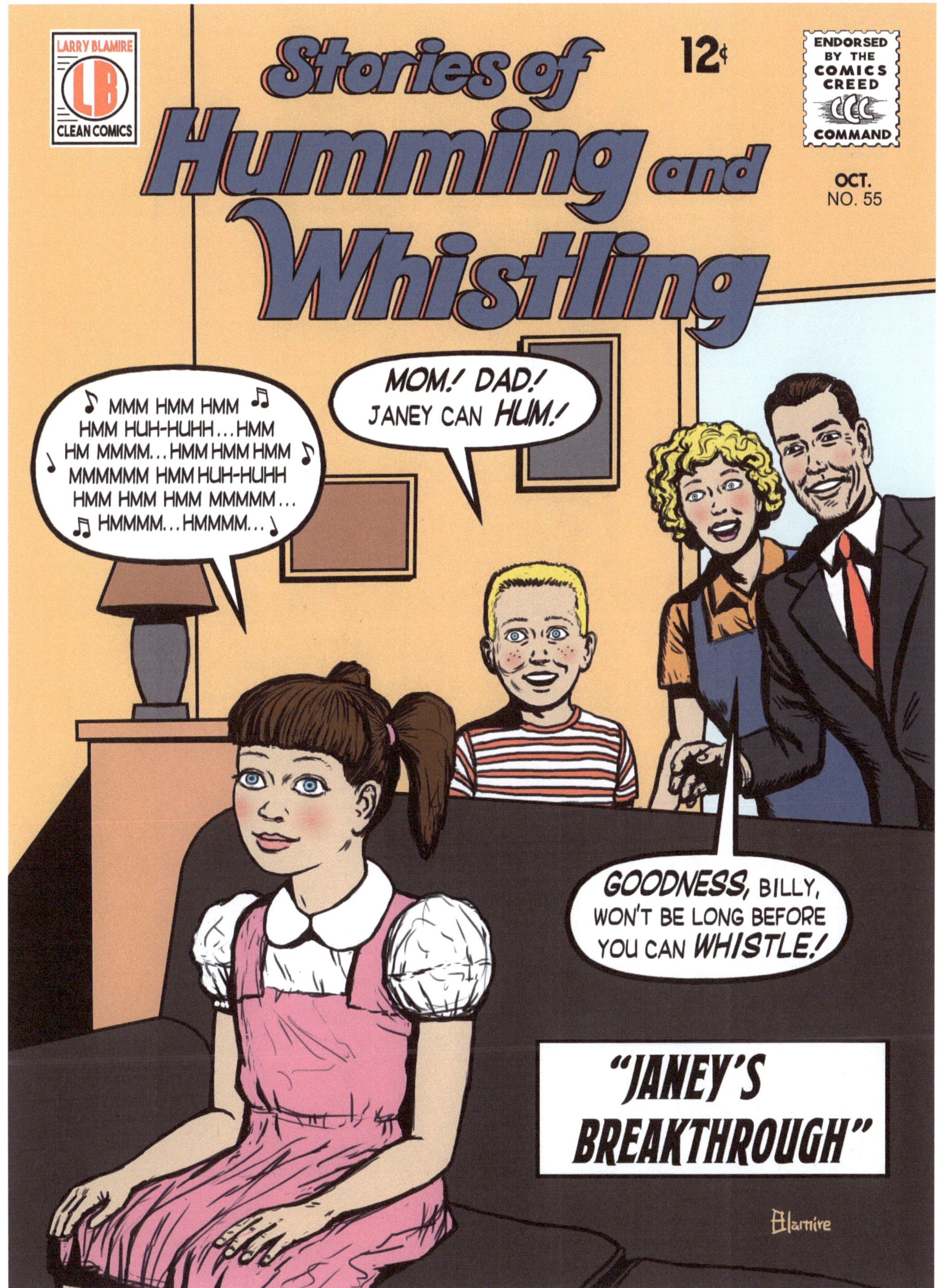
LARRY BLAMIRE
LB
CLEAN COMICS
Stories of Humming and Whistling
12¢
ENDORSED BY THE COMICS CREED
CCC
COMMAND
OCT.
NO. 55
MMM HMM HMM HMM HUH-HUHH...HMM HM MMMM...HMM HMM HMM MMMMMM HMM HUH-HUHH HMM HMM HMM MMMMM... HMMMM...HMMMM...
MOM! DAD! JANEY CAN HUM!
GOODNESS, BILLY, WON'T BE LONG BEFORE YOU CAN WHISTLE!
"JANEY'S BREAKTHROUGH"
Blamire

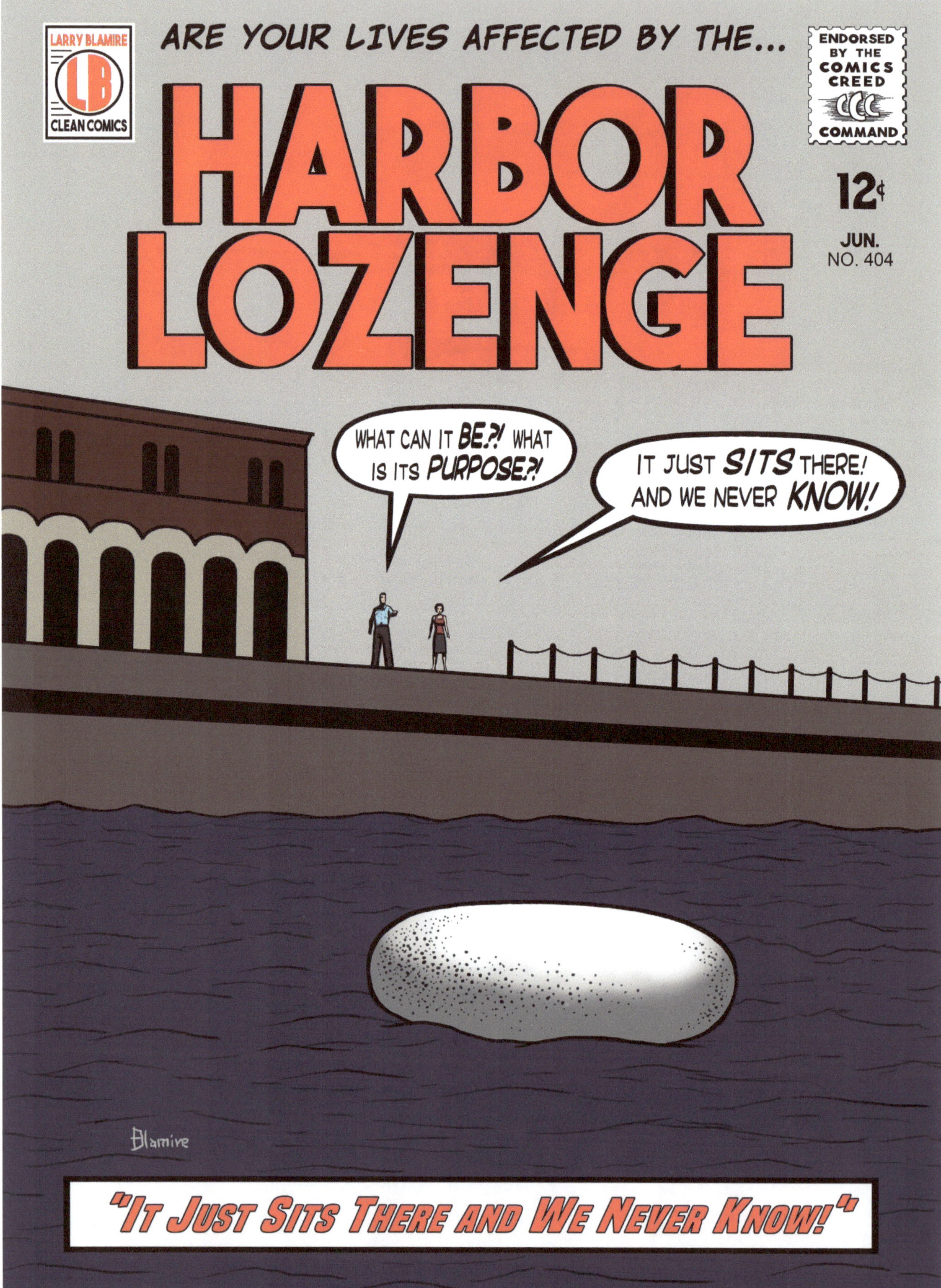
LARRY BLAMIRE
LB
CLEAN COMICS
ARE YOUR LIVES AFFECTED BY THE...
HARBOR LOZENGE
ENDORSED BY THE COMICS CREED
CCC
COMMAND
12¢
JUN.
NO. 404
WHAT CAN IT BE.?! WHAT IS ITS PURPOSE.?!
IT JUST SITS THERE! AND WE NEVER KNOW!
Blamire
"IT JUST SITS THERE AND WE NEVER KNOW!"

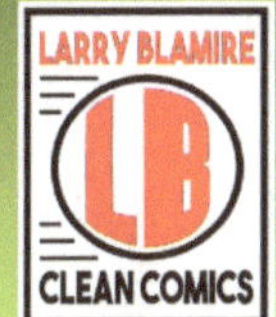

THE COMIC BOOK OF FUNNY HUMOR

12¢

WHOOPS

MAR.
NO. 6

With your proprietor HILTON T. LOOTIS

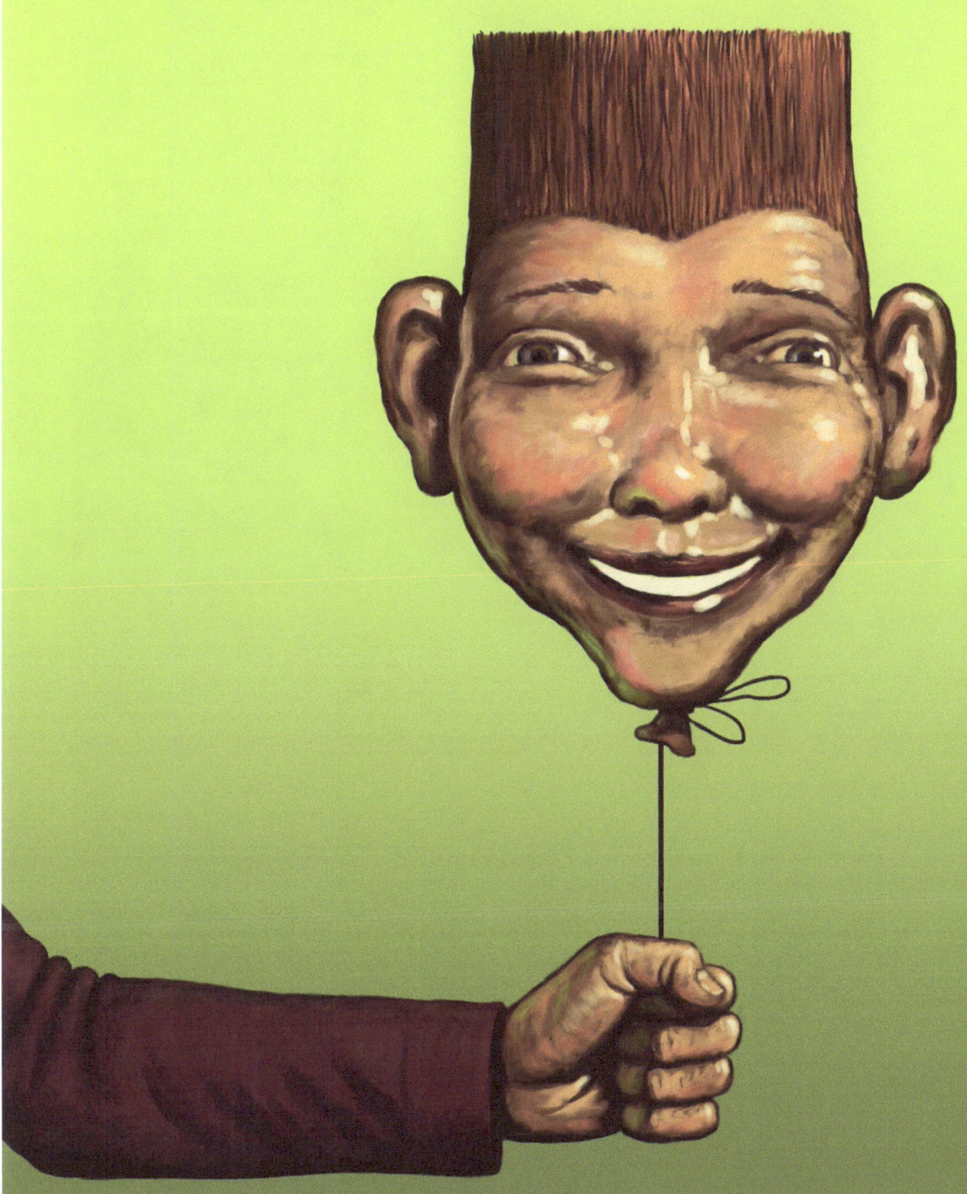

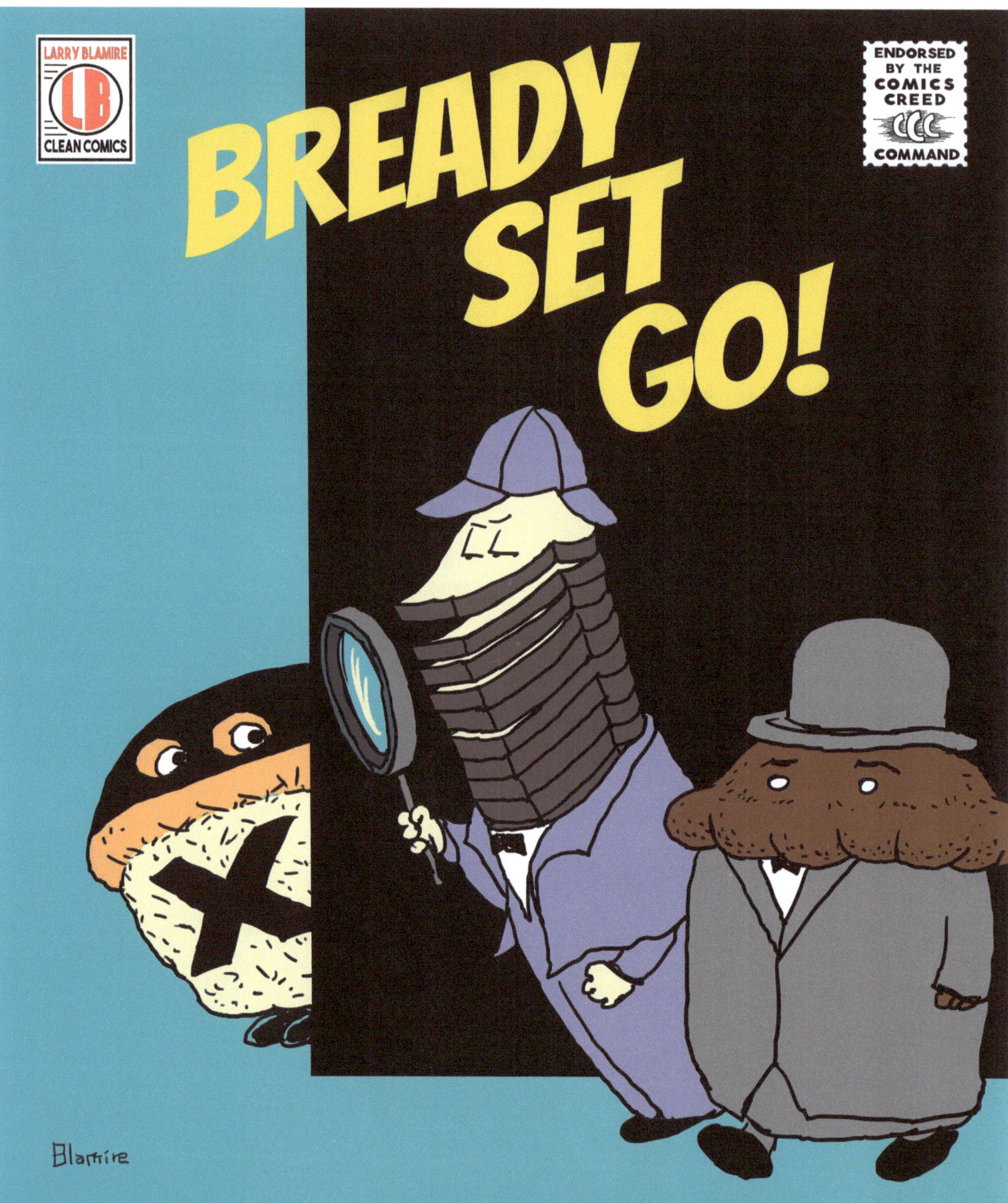

CRUST NO ONE! SHERLOAF AND DR. MUFFIN TRACK DOWN THE MYSTERIOUS ROLL X!

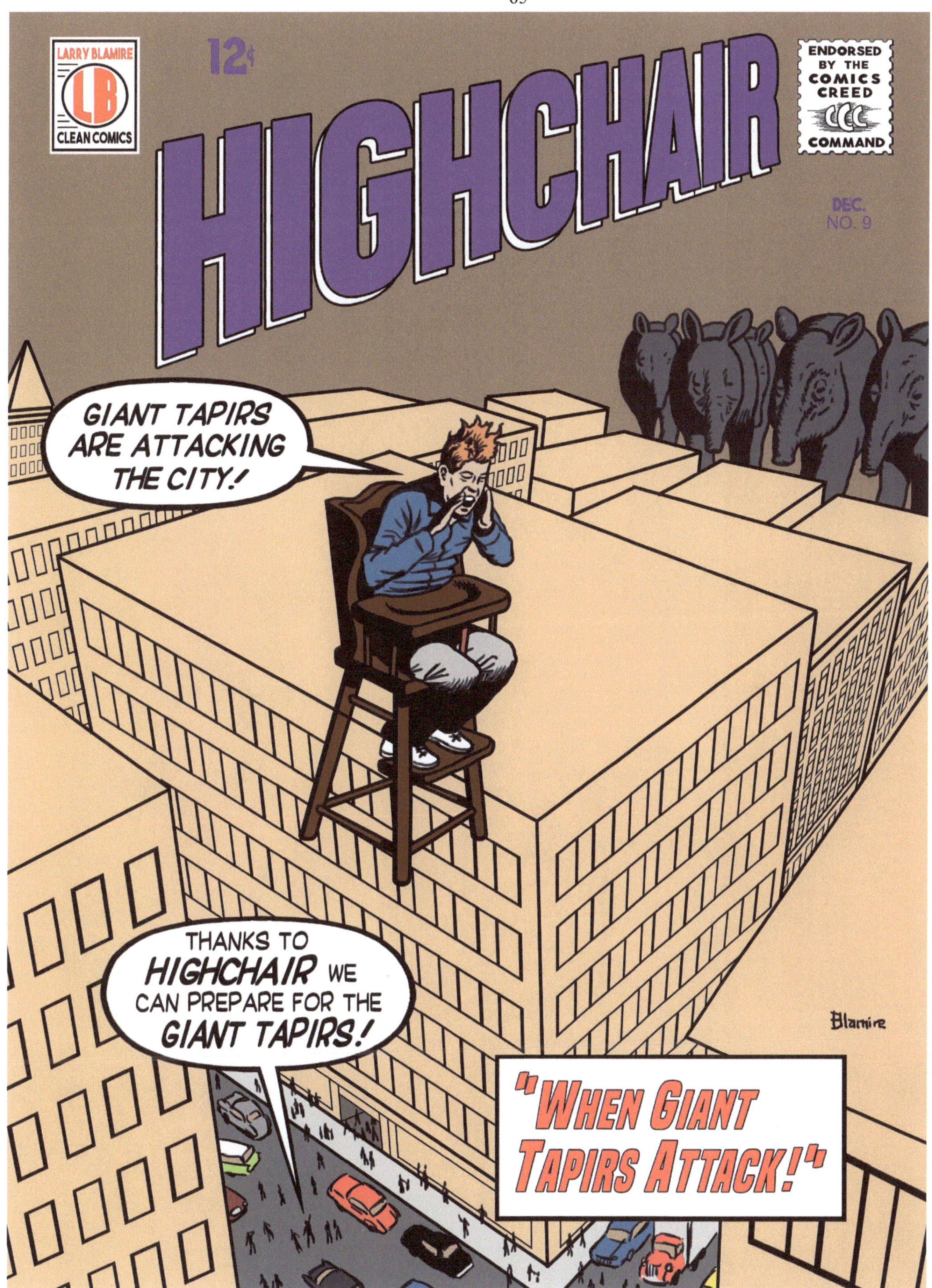
LARRY BLAMIRE
LB
CLEAN COMICS
12¢
HIGHCHAIR
ENDORSED BY THE COMICS CREED
CCC
COMMAND
DEC.
NO. 9
GIANT TAPIRS ARE ATTACKING THE CITY!
THANKS TO HIGHCHAIR WE CAN PREPARE FOR THE GIANT TAPIRS!
Blamire
"WHEN GIANT TAPIRS ATTACK!"

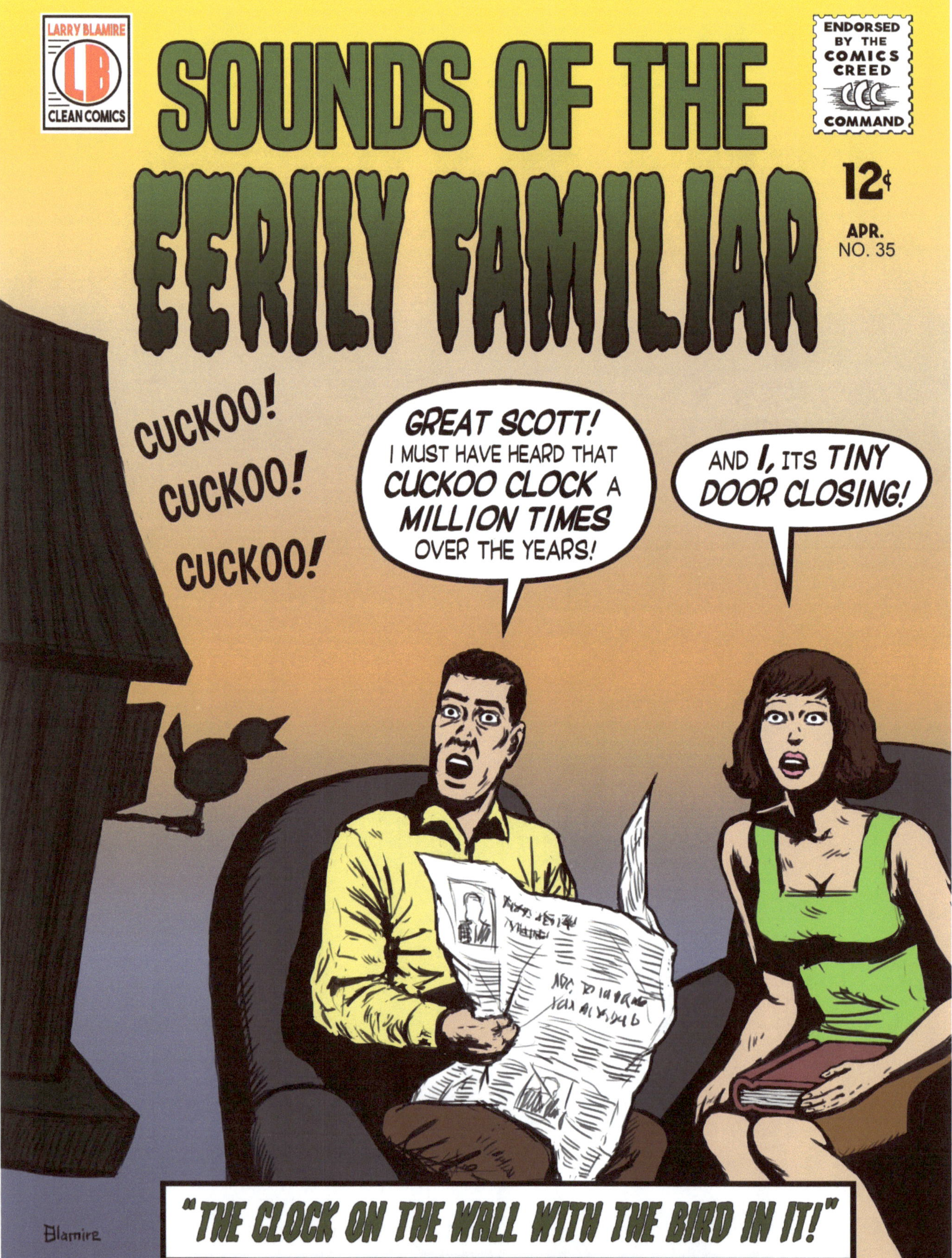
LARRY BLAMIRE
LB
CLEAN COMICS
SOUNDS OF THE
EERILY FAMILIAR
ENDORSED BY THE COMICS CREED
CCC
COMMAND
12¢
APR.
NO. 35
CUCKOO!
CUCKOO!
CUCKOO!
GREAT SCOTT! I MUST HAVE HEARD THAT CUCKOO CLOCK A MILLION TIMES OVER THE YEARS!
AND I, ITS TINY DOOR CLOSING!
"THE CLOCK ON THE WALL WITH THE BIRD IN IT!"
Blamire

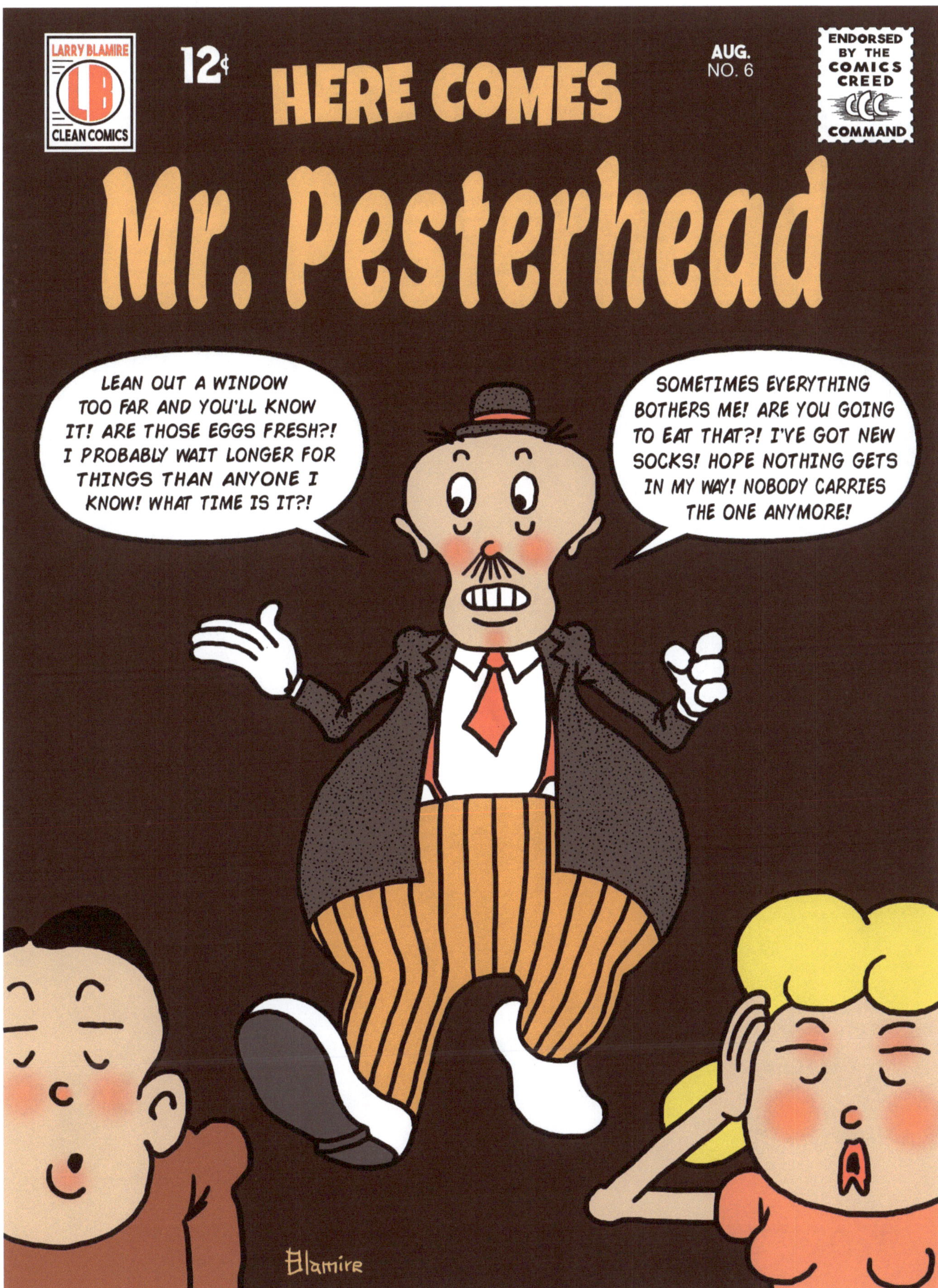
LARRY BLAMIRE
LB
CLEAN COMICS
12¢
HERE COMES
AUG.
NO. 6
ENDORSED BY THE COMICS CREED
CCC
COMMAND
Mr. Pesterhead
LEAN OUT A WINDOW TOO FAR AND YOU'LL KNOW IT! ARE THOSE EGGS FRESH?! I PROBABLY WAIT LONGER FOR THINGS THAN ANYONE I KNOW! WHAT TIME IS IT?!
SOMETIMES EVERYTHING BOTHERS ME! ARE YOU GOING TO EAT THAT?! I'VE GOT NEW SOCKS! HOPE NOTHING GETS IN MY WAY! NOBODY CARRIES THE ONE ANYMORE!
Blamire

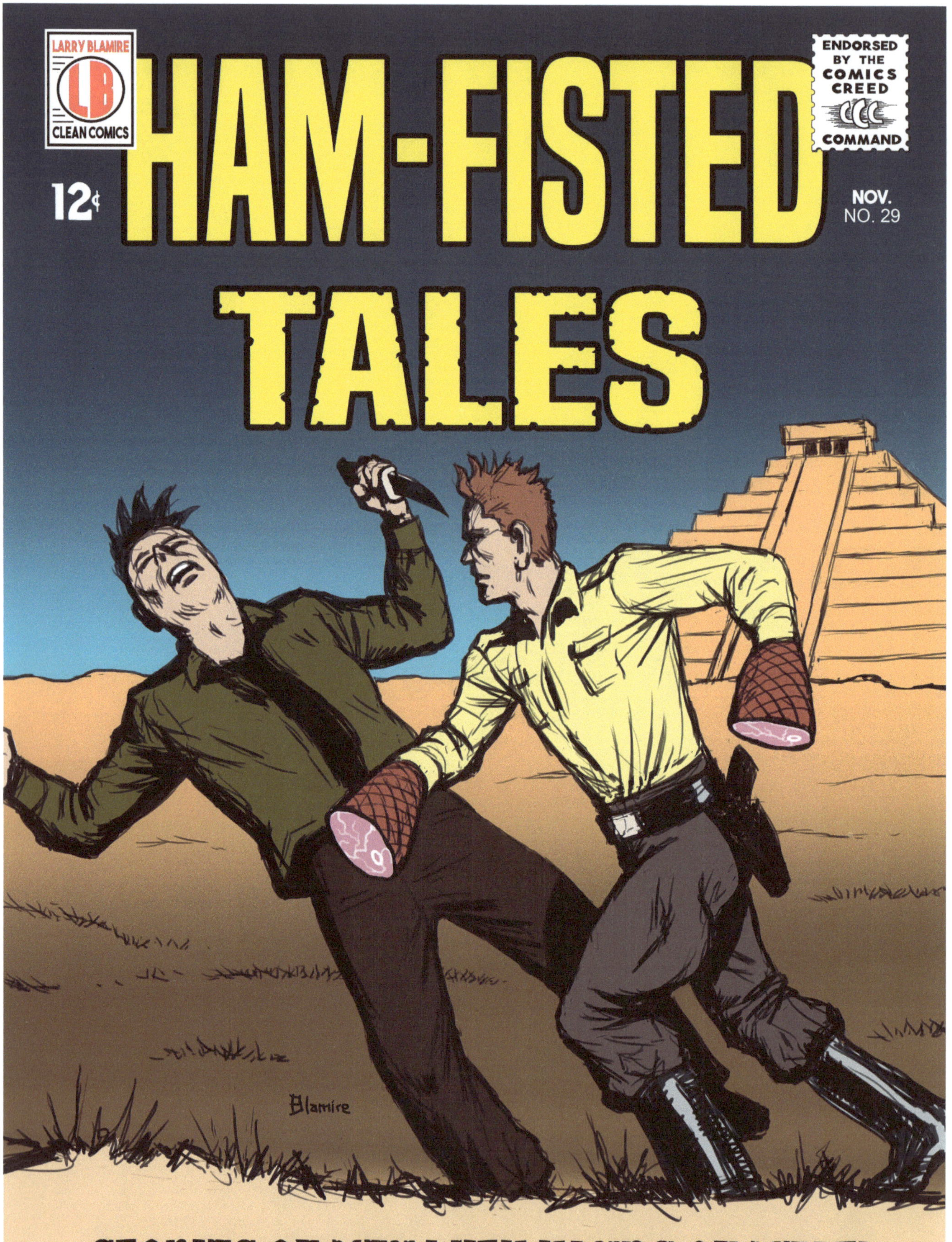
LARRY BLAMIRE
LB
CLEAN COMICS
HAM-FISTED
TALES
12¢
ENDORSED BY THE COMICS CREED
CCC
COMMAND
NOV.
NO. 29
Blamire
STORIES OF MEN WITH HANDS OF MEAT!

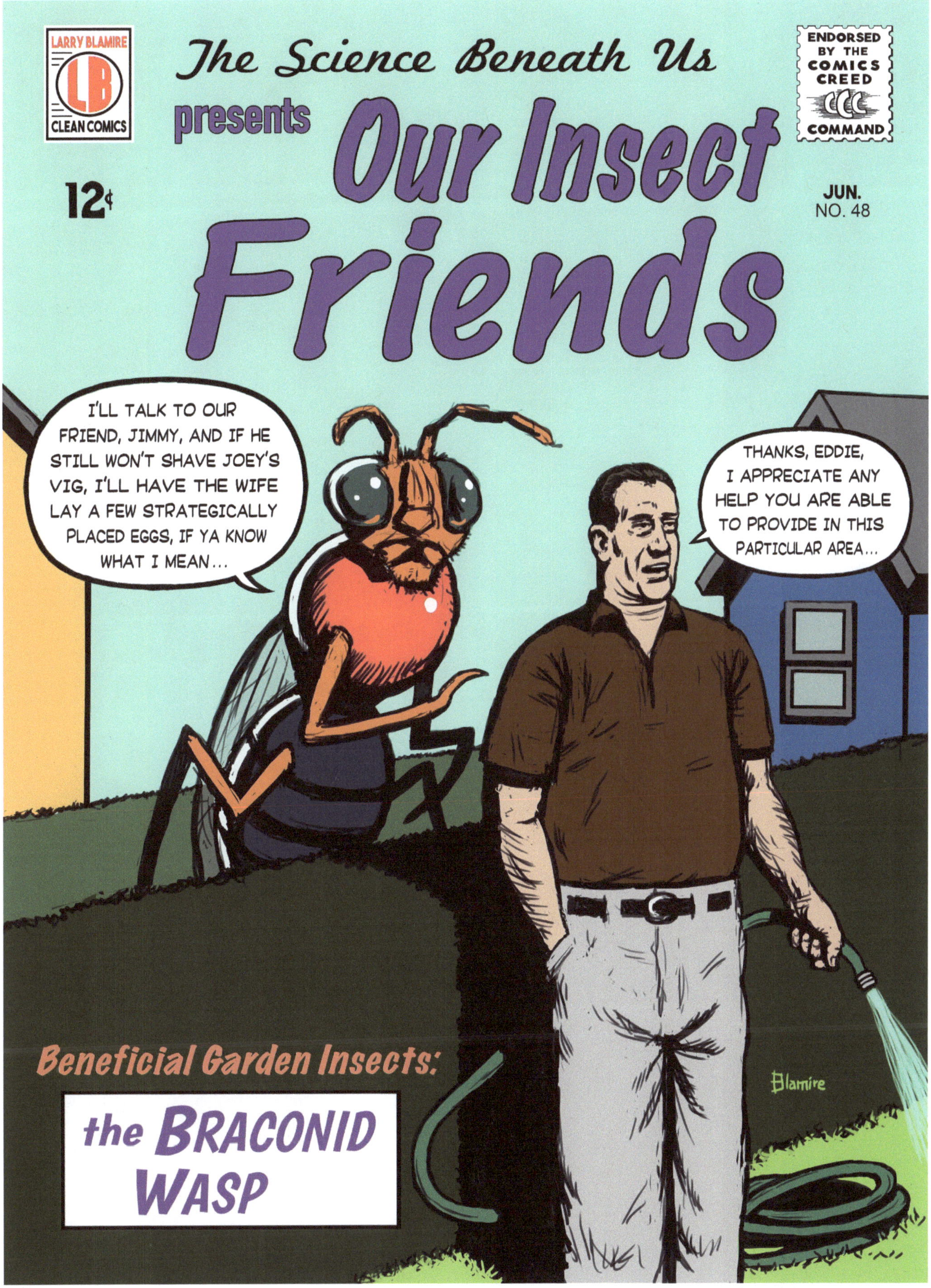

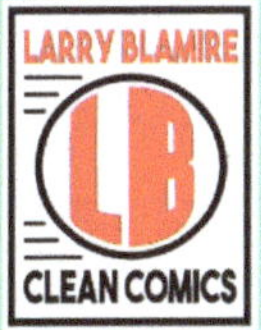

The Science Beneath Us

presents

Our Insect Friends

12¢

ENDORSED BY THE COMICS CREED COMMAND

JUN.
NO. 48

I'LL TALK TO OUR FRIEND, JIMMY, AND IF HE STILL WON'T SHAVE JOEY'S VIG, I'LL HAVE THE WIFE LAY A FEW STRATEGICALLY PLACED EGGS, IF YA KNOW WHAT I MEAN...

THANKS, EDDIE, I APPRECIATE ANY HELP YOU ARE ABLE TO PROVIDE IN THIS PARTICULAR AREA...

Blamire

Beneficial Garden Insects:

the BRACONID WASP

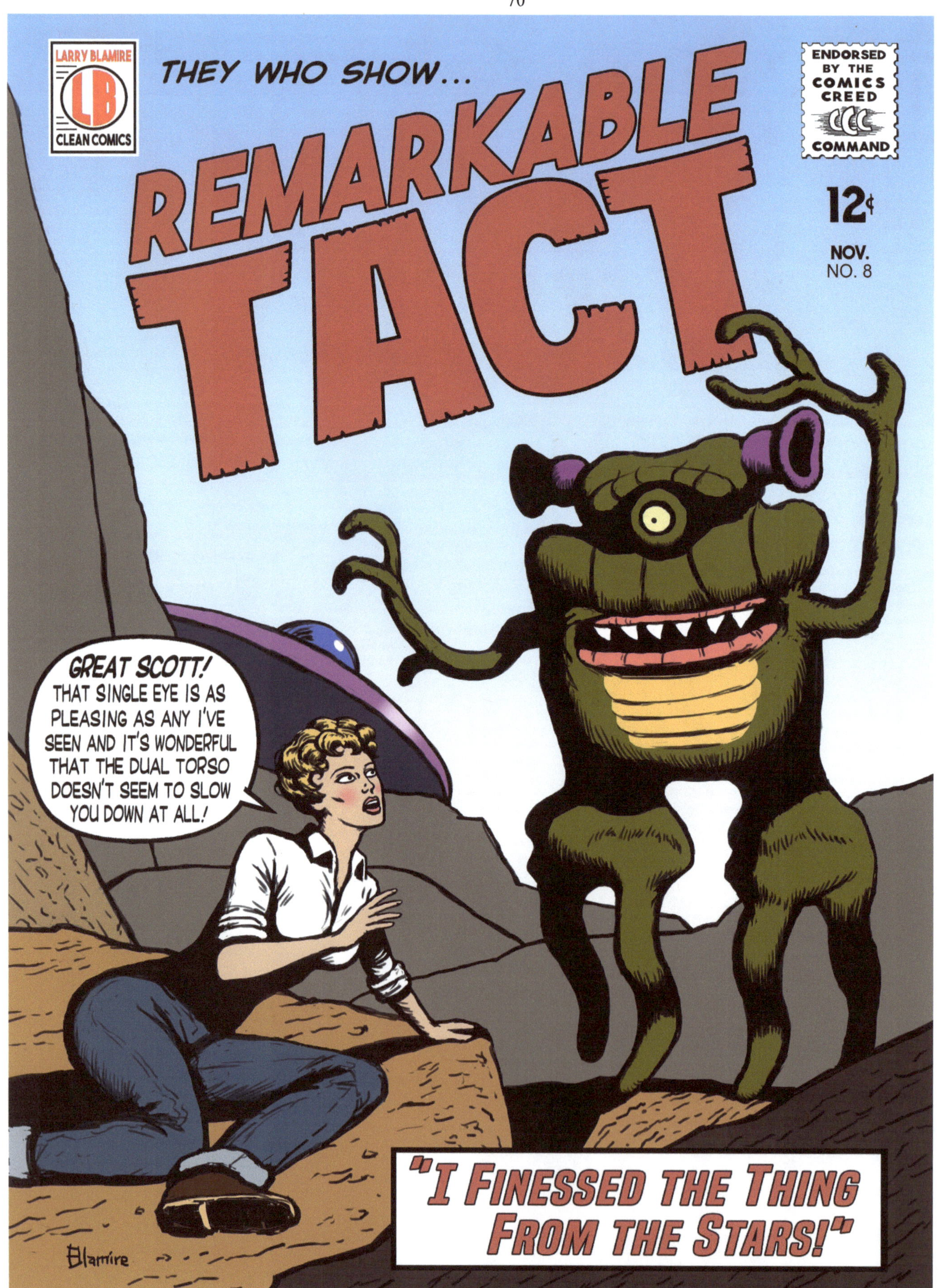
LARRY BLAMIRE
LB
CLEAN COMICS
THEY WHO SHOW...
REMARKABLE TACT
ENDORSED BY THE COMICS CREED
CCC
COMMAND
12¢
NOV.
NO. 8
GREAT SCOTT! THAT SINGLE EYE IS AS PLEASING AS ANY I'VE SEEN AND IT'S WONDERFUL THAT THE DUAL TORSO DOESN'T SEEM TO SLOW YOU DOWN AT ALL!
"I FINESSED THE THING FROM THE STARS!"
Blamire

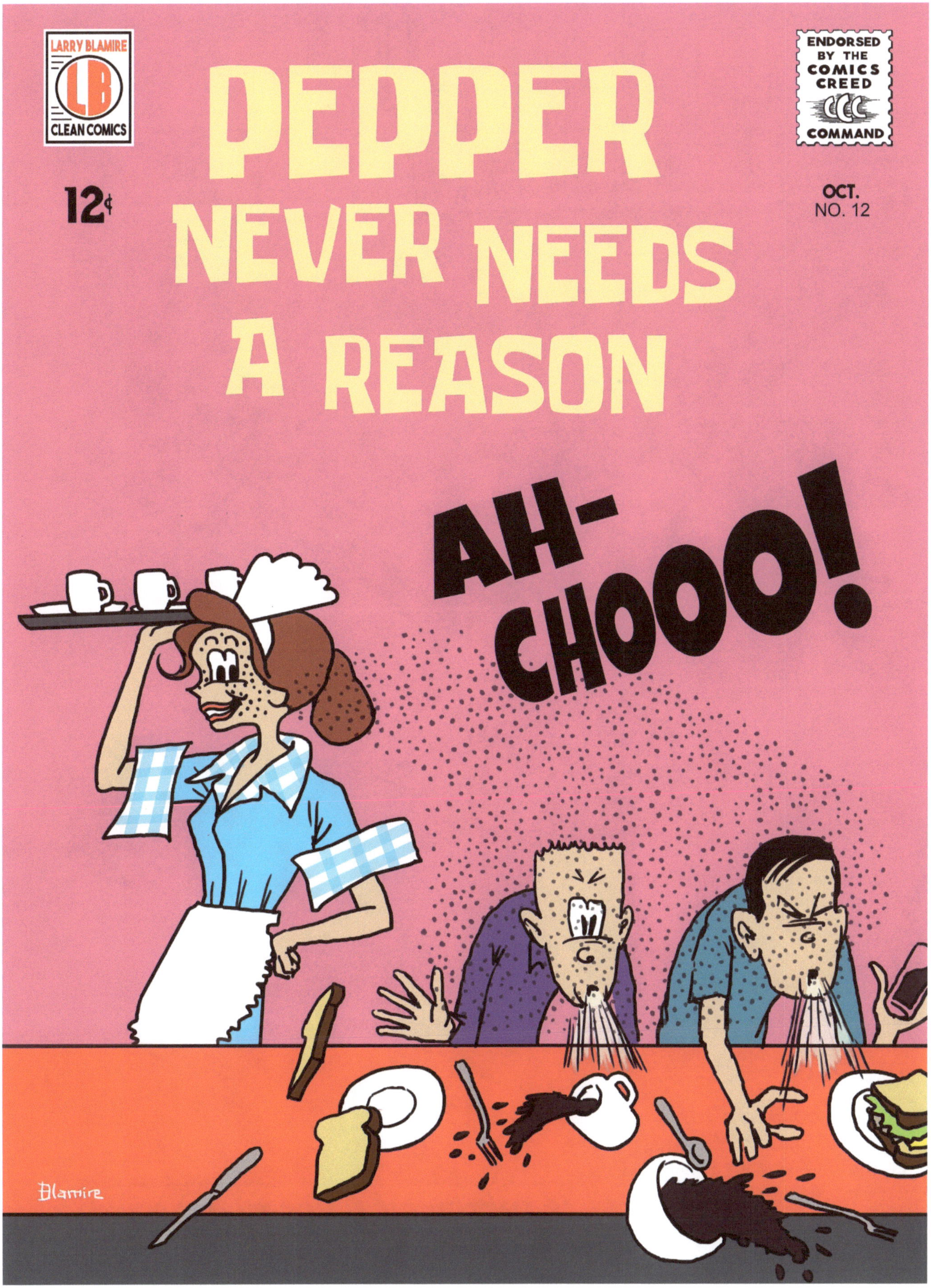

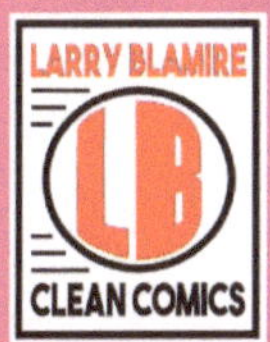

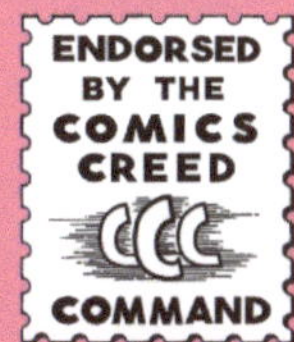

PEPPER NEVER NEEDS A REASON

12¢

OCT.
NO. 12

AH-
CHOOO!

Blamire

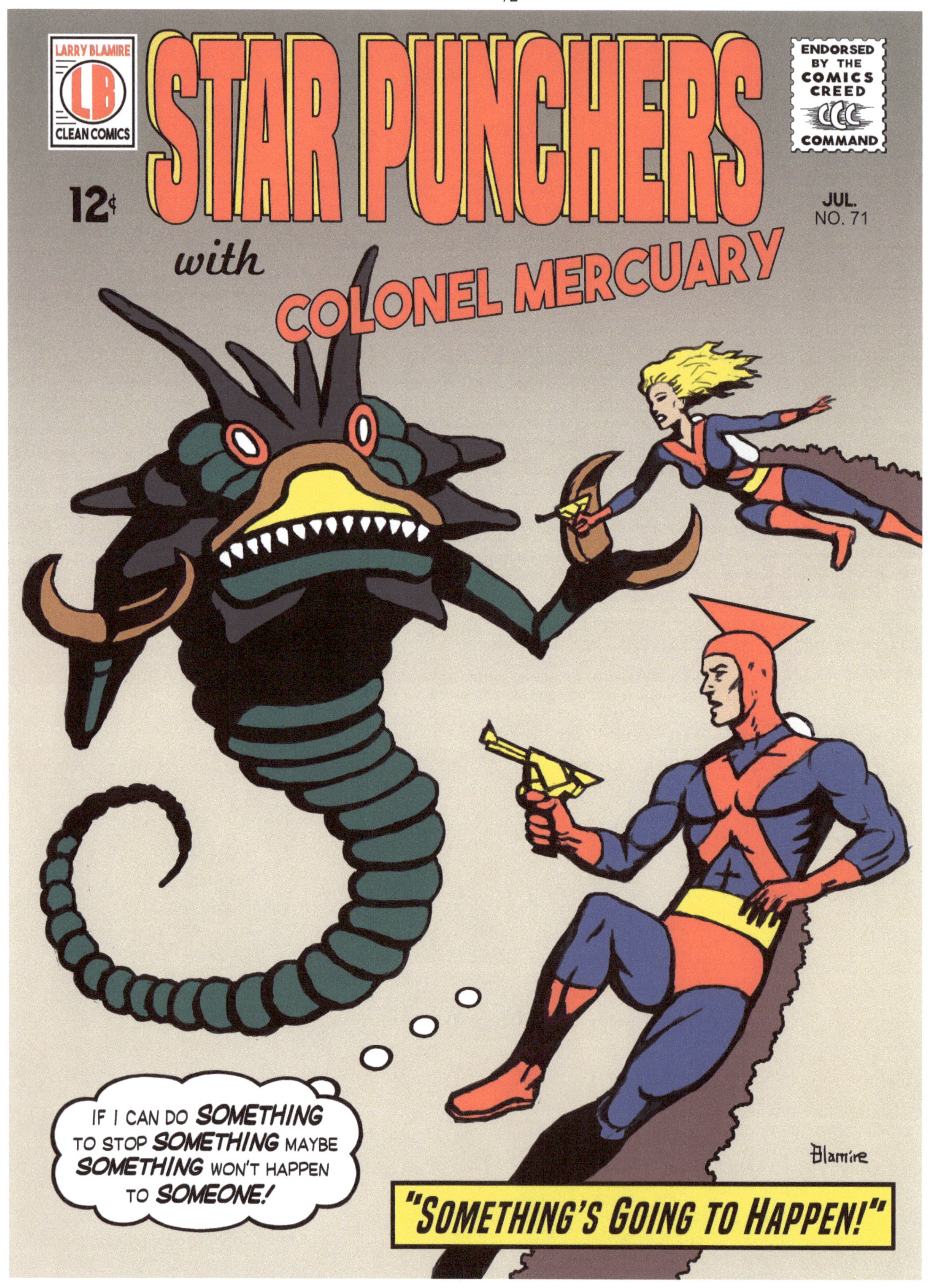
LARRY BLAMIRE
LB
CLEAN COMICS
STAR PUNCHERS
ENDORSED BY THE COMICS CREED
CCC
COMMAND
12¢
JUL.
NO. 71
with COLONEL MERCUARY
IF I CAN DO SOMETHING TO STOP SOMETHING MAYBE SOMETHING WON'T HAPPEN TO SOMEONE!
Blamire
"SOMETHING'S GOING TO HAPPEN!"

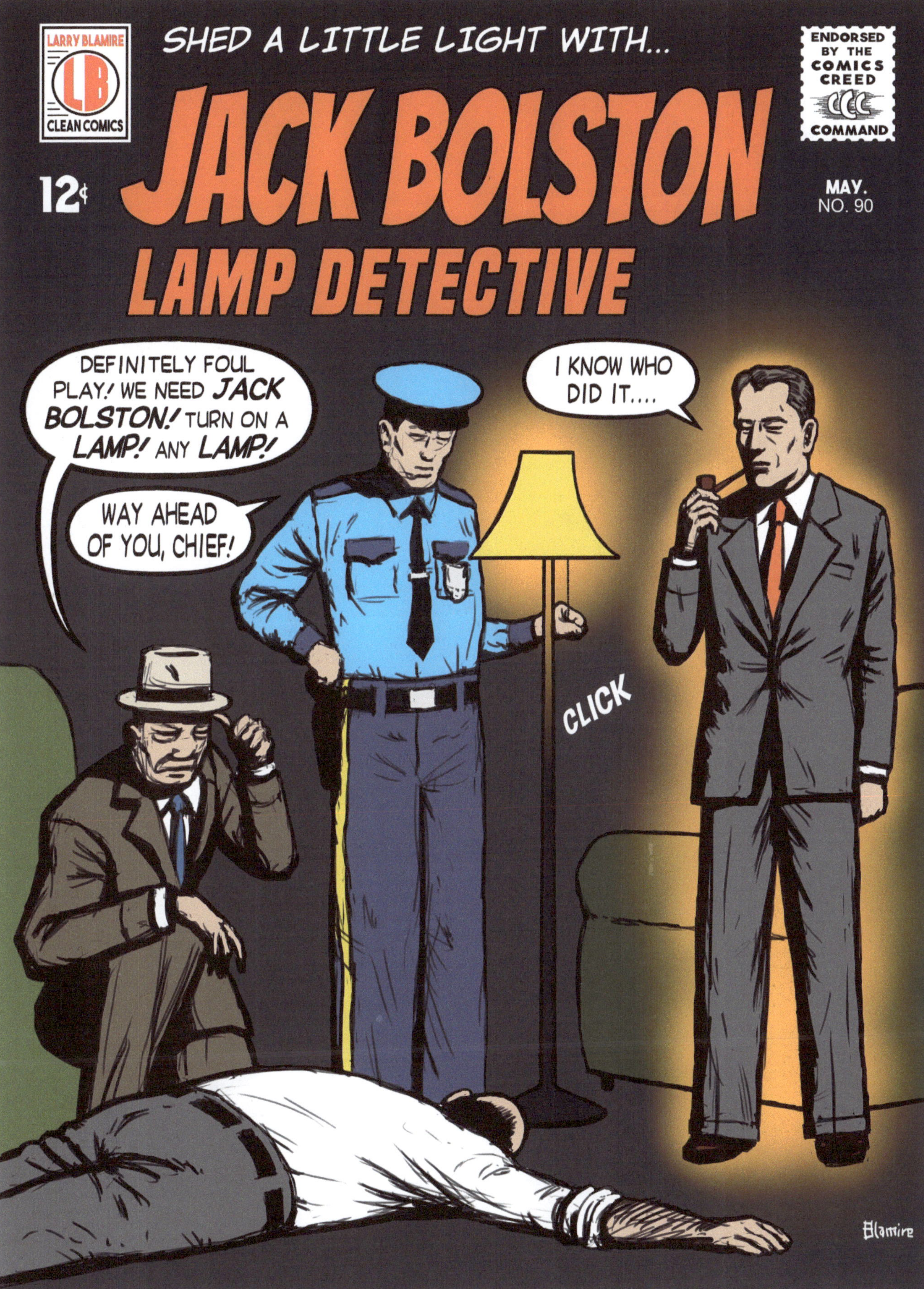
LARRY BLAMIRE
LB
CLEAN COMICS
SHED A LITTLE LIGHT WITH...
JACK BOLSTON
LAMP DETECTIVE
ENDORSED BY THE COMICS CREED
CCC
COMMAND
12¢
MAY.
NO. 90
DEFINITELY FOUL PLAY! WE NEED JACK BOLSTON! TURN ON A LAMP! ANY LAMP!
WAY AHEAD OF YOU, CHIEF!
CLICK
I KNOW WHO DID IT....
Blamire

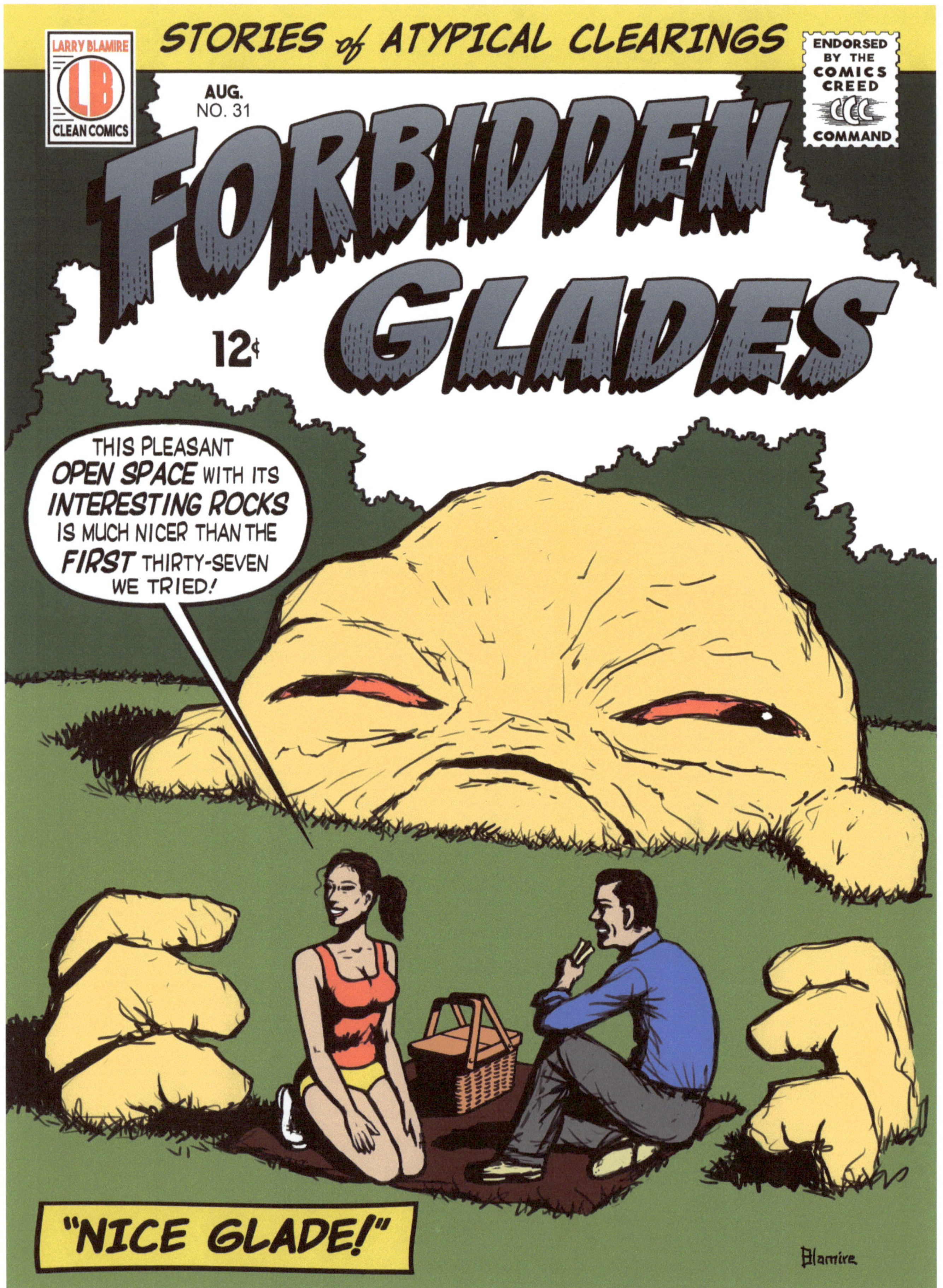
STORIES of ATYPICAL CLEARINGS
LARRY BLAMIRE
LB
CLEAN COMICS
ENDORSED BY THE COMICS CREED
CCC
COMMAND
AUG.
NO. 31
FORBIDDEN GLADES
12¢
THIS PLEASANT OPEN SPACE WITH ITS INTERESTING ROCKS IS MUCH NICER THAN THE FIRST THIRTY-SEVEN WE TRIED!
"NICE GLADE!"
Blamire

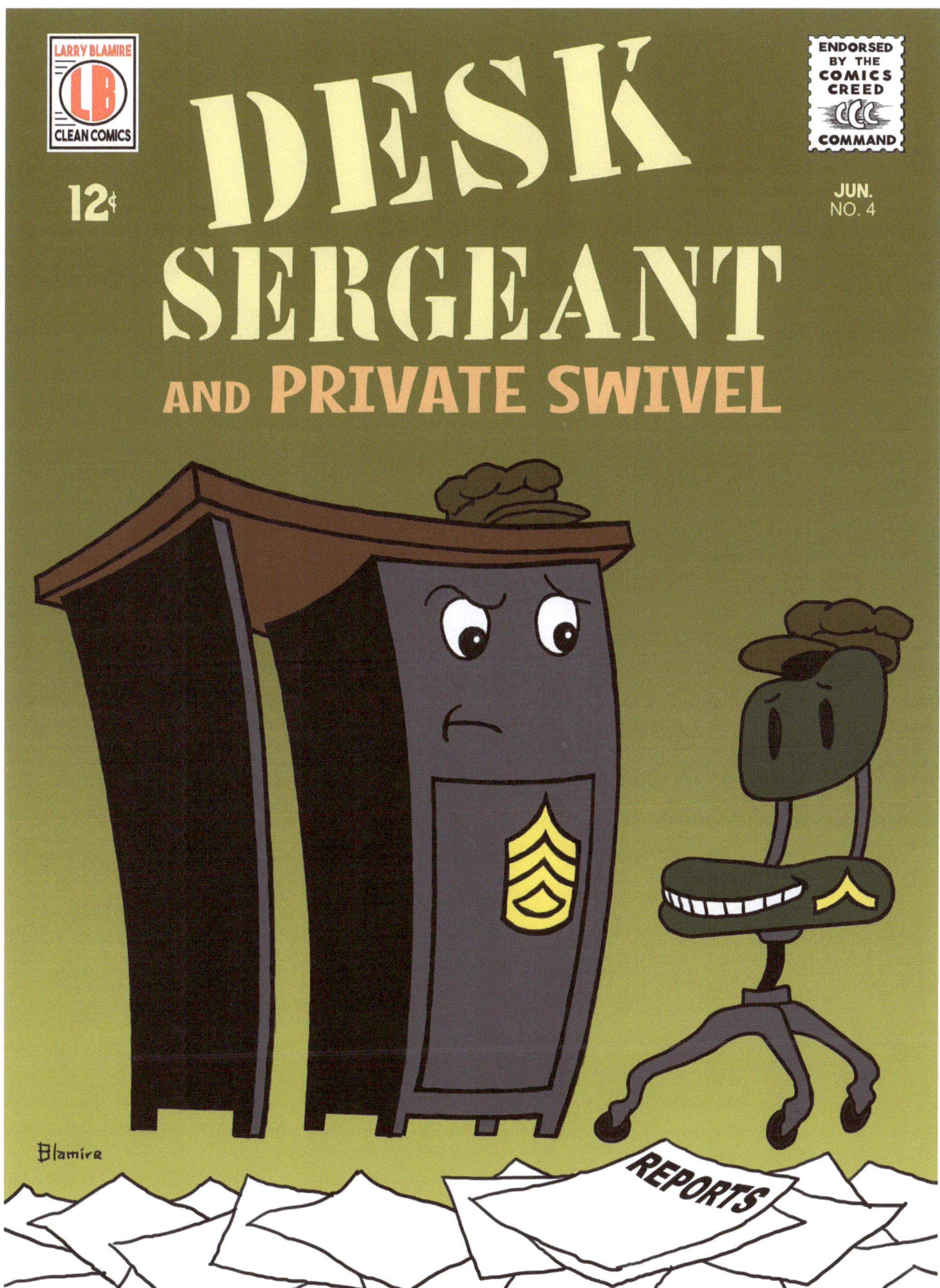
LARRY BLAMIRE
LB
CLEAN COMICS
DESK SERGEANT
AND PRIVATE SWIVEL
ENDORSED BY THE COMICS CREED
CCC
COMMAND
12¢
JUN.
NO. 4
Blamire
REPORTS

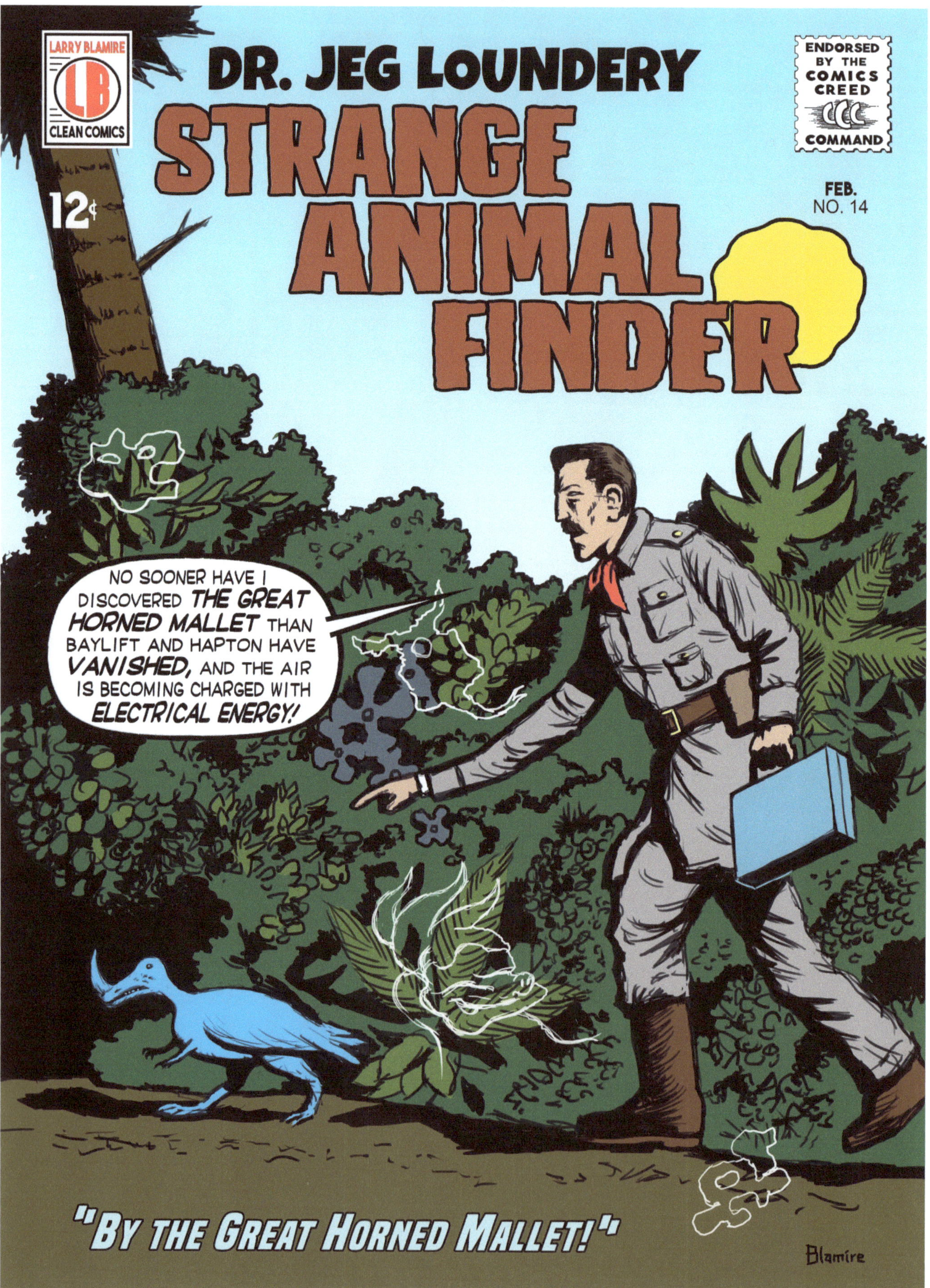
LARRY BLAMIRE
LB
CLEAN COMICS
12¢
DR. JEG LOUNDERY
STRANGE ANIMAL FINDER
ENDORSED BY THE COMICS CREED
CCC
COMMAND
FEB.
NO. 14
NO SOONER HAVE I DISCOVERED THE GREAT HORNED MALLET THAN BAYLIFT AND HAPTON HAVE VANISHED, AND THE AIR IS BECOMING CHARGED WITH ELECTRICAL ENERGY!
"BY THE GREAT HORNED MALLET!"
Blamire

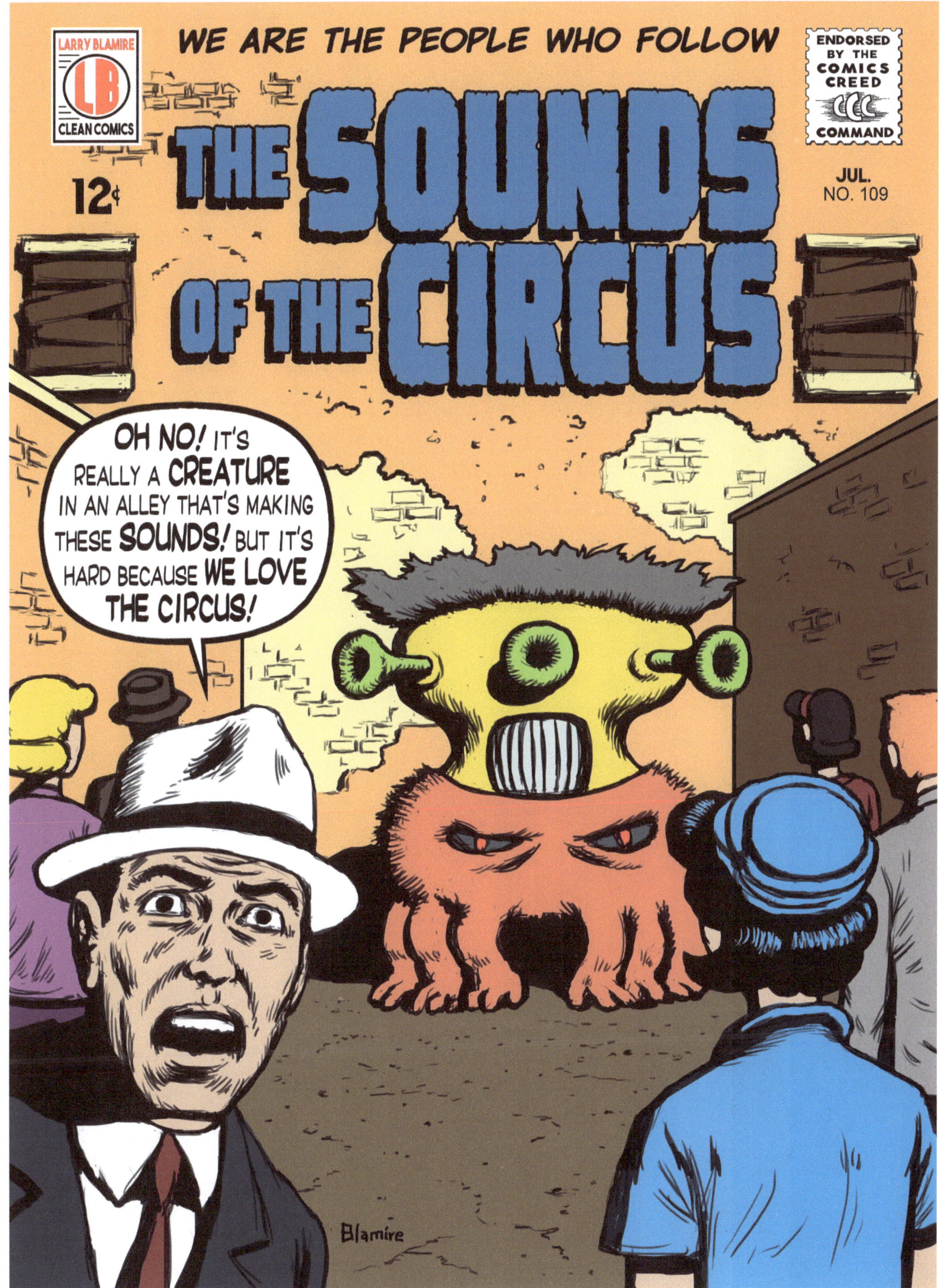
LARRY BLAMIRE
LB
CLEAN COMICS
WE ARE THE PEOPLE WHO FOLLOW
ENDORSED BY THE COMICS CREED
CCC
COMMAND
THE SOUNDS OF THE CIRCUS
12¢
JUL.
NO. 109
OH NO! IT'S REALLY A CREATURE IN AN ALLEY THAT'S MAKING THESE SOUNDS! BUT IT'S HARD BECAUSE WE LOVE THE CIRCUS!
Blamire

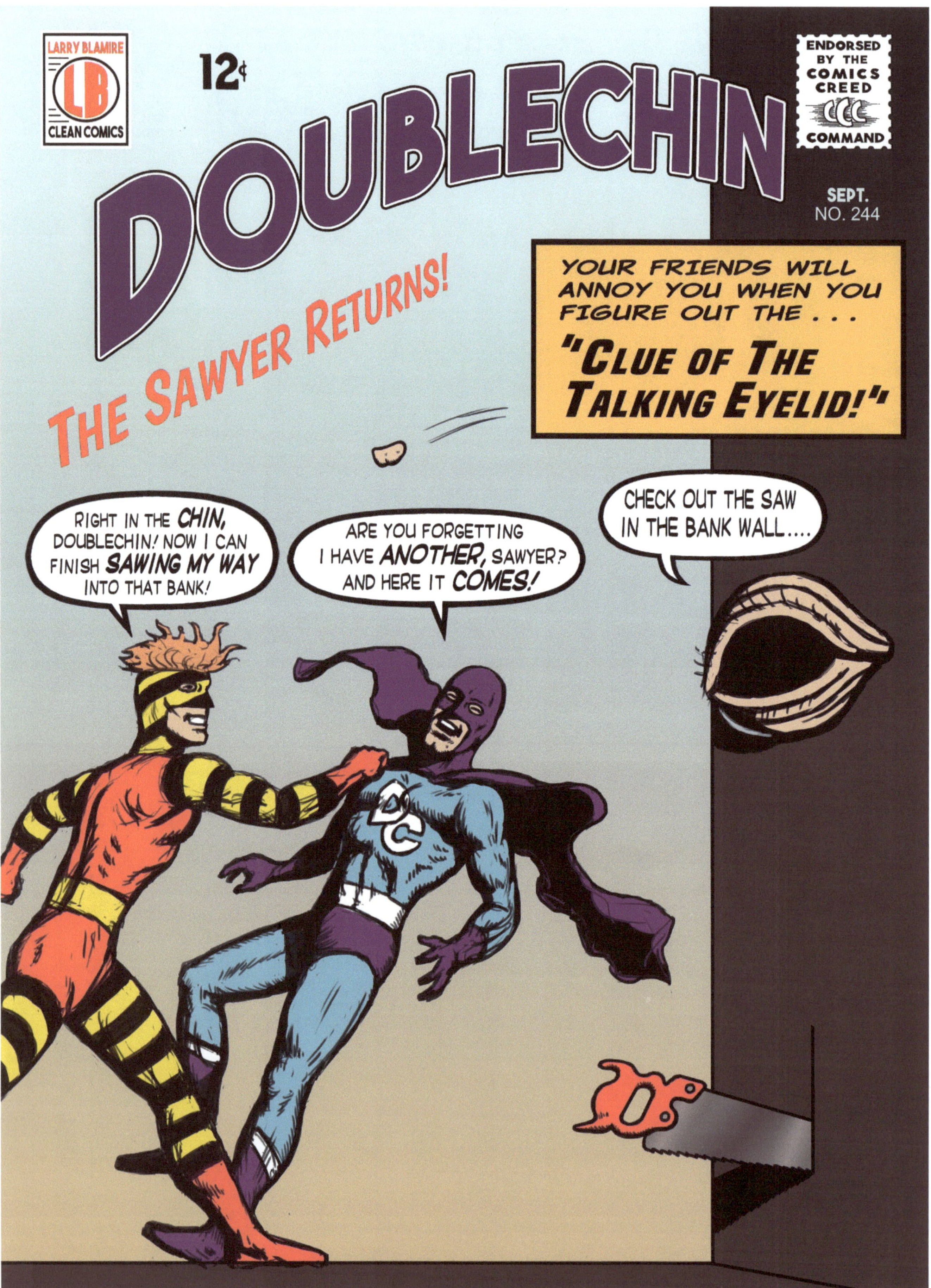
LARRY BLAMIRE
LB
CLEAN COMICS
12¢
DOUBLECHIN
ENDORSED BY THE COMICS CREED
CCC
COMMAND
SEPT.
NO. 244
THE SAWYER RETURNS!
YOUR FRIENDS WILL ANNOY YOU WHEN YOU FIGURE OUT THE . . .
"CLUE OF THE TALKING EYELID!"
RIGHT IN THE CHIN, DOUBLECHIN! NOW I CAN FINISH SAWING MY WAY INTO THAT BANK!
ARE YOU FORGETTING I HAVE ANOTHER, SAWYER? AND HERE IT COMES!
CHECK OUT THE SAW IN THE BANK WALL....
DC

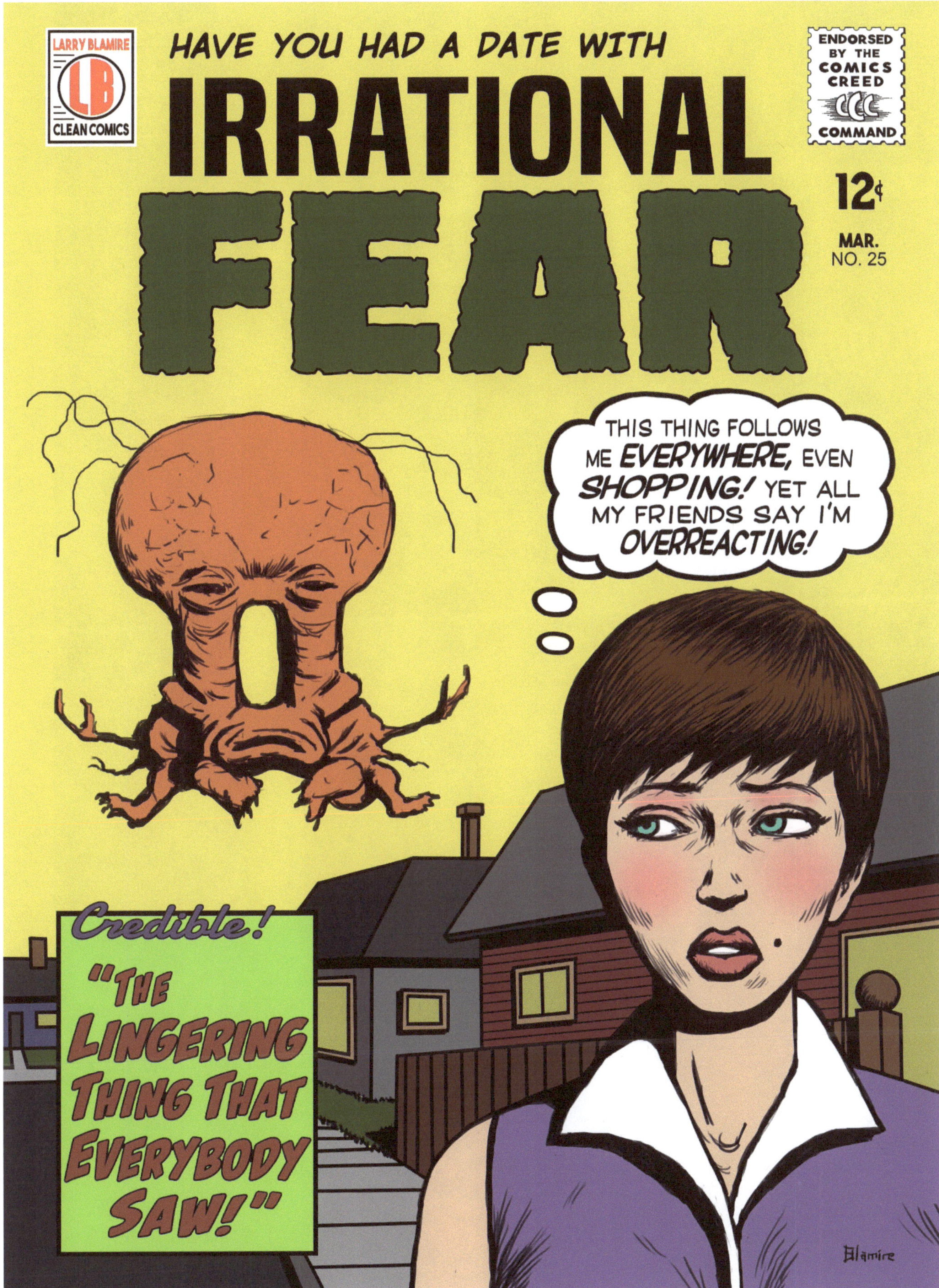
LARRY BLAMIRE
LB
CLEAN COMICS
HAVE YOU HAD A DATE WITH
IRRATIONAL
FEAR
ENDORSED BY THE COMICS CREED
CCC
COMMAND
12¢
MAR.
NO. 25
THIS THING FOLLOWS ME EVERYWHERE, EVEN SHOPPING! YET ALL MY FRIENDS SAY I'M OVERREACTING!
Credible!
"THE LINGERING THING THAT EVERYBODY SAW!"
Blamire

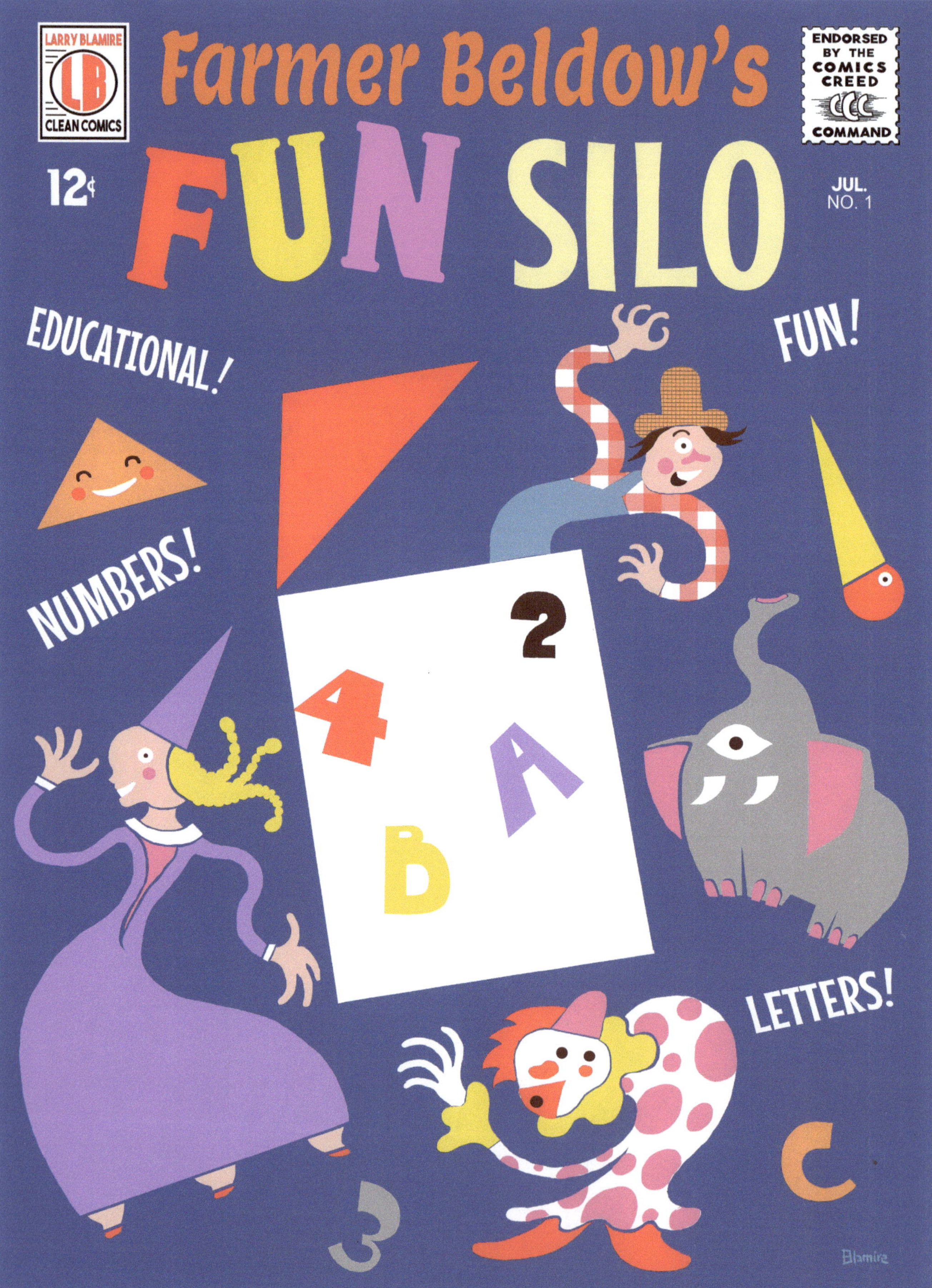
LARRY BLAMIRE
LB
CLEAN COMICS
Farmer Beldow's
ENDORSED BY THE COMICS CREED
CCC
COMMAND
12¢
FUN SILO
JUL.
NO. 1
EDUCATIONAL!
FUN!
NUMBERS!
2
4
A
B
LETTERS!
C
3
Blamire

www.ingramcontent.com/pod-product-compliance
Lightning Source LLC
LaVergne TN
LVHW070508120826
845147LV00031BA/258
9780692189184